MARI
LAW
FOR BOAT OWNERS

Other Titles of Interest

All at Sea: A collection of marine legal stories   Clive Ward
ISBN 0 7136 3753 6

How often does one read in the yachting press of substandard workmanship, negligence on the part of boatyards, wrangles over salvage claims, late deliveries, breaches of contract, unwitting purchases of stolen boats and faulty surveyors' reports? This collection of stories makes fascinating reading on a subject close to any boat owner's heart.

How to Choose the Right Yacht   Joachim F Muhs
ISBN 0 7136 3950 4

Many yachts at boat shows look almost identical, so how can a prospective buyer judge a yacht's sailing abilities from the sales brochures alone? This book shows how interested buyers can assess whether a boat is fast or slow, wet or dry, holds its course well and many other things – all from the comfort of their own home.

Trailer Sailing   J C Winters
ISBN 0 7136 3779 X

Trailer sailing comes close to the ideal for many sailors, combining as it does the freedom to sail where you like whenever you like at reasonable cost. The book offers a comprehensive insight into all aspects of this sport and will enable readers to hitch up and set off to hitherto unexplored waters.

Through the French Canals 8th edition   Philip Bristow
ISBN 0 7136 3844 3

The new edition of this bestselling cruising guide includes new photographs and practical information on local facilities, distances, heights and depths which will be invaluable to anyone planning a cruise on the French waterways or on passage from the English Channel through to the Mediterranean.

First Aid at Sea 2nd edition   Douglas Justins and Colin Berry
ISBN 0 7136 3826 5

The new edition of this invaluable on-board reference has a colour coded thumb index of emergencies, concise descriptions of medical conditions with a prioritised list of treatments, checklist for quick access and is laminated and spiral bound to withstand weather.

Total Loss   Jack Coote
ISBN 0 7136 3613 0

Now available in paperback, *Total Loss* is an anthology of carefully selected accounts by well known authors who have suffered a loss at sea. The stories are grouped under the principal causes of loss and each is followed by an analysis of the lessons to be learned.

MARINE LAW
FOR BOAT OWNERS

Edmund Whelan

Adlard Coles Nautical
London

This edition published in 1994 by Adlard Coles Nautical
an imprint of A & C Black (Publishers) Ltd
35 Bedford Row, London WC1R 4JH

First edition 1994

ISBN 0-7136-3911-3

A CIP catalogue record for this book is available from the
British Library.

Typeset in 10/11pt Linotron Palatino by Falcon Graphic
Arts, Wallington, Surrey.
Printed and bound in Great Britain by Cromwell Press

CONTENTS

1 *OWNERSHIP & REGISTRATION OF A YACHT* 1
Requirement to register 1
Owning a ship 4
Legal and beneficial ownership 5
Registration in the United Kingdom 5
Formalities of registration 6
Creation and registration of mortgages 12

2 *BUYING & SELLING A SECOND-HAND YACHT* 14
The contract 15
The survey 19
Checking the vendor's title 21
Unregistered mortgages 22
VAT liabilities 23
Formalities on completion 24
Disputes after completion 25

3 *BUYING A NEW YACHT* 28
Boats built to special order 28
Buying from stock 33
Purchasing through an agent 35
Other matters in the contract 36
Buying for overseas delivery 36

4 *CONSTRUCTION & EQUIPMENT REGULATIONS* 39
Inland waterways regulations 39
Department of Transport rules for pleasure craft
   used commercially 43
European Council Directive on Recreational Craft 47

5   CONSUMER PROTECTION   50
    Repair and conversion   50
    Statutory consumer protection   52
    Taking legal proceedings   60

6   RULES OF THE ROAD & COLLISIONS   64
    Special position of racing yachts   67
    Proving fault   68
    Defences   68
    Contributory negligence   69
    Principles of compensation   72
    Limitation of liability   73

7   PUBLIC RIGHTS OF NAVIGATION   76
    Consents required for providing moorings in tidal waters   78
    Restrictions on navigation rights   80

8   FLAG LAW   89
    Privileged ensigns   90
    Prevention of abuse   92
    The European Community   93

9   INSURANCE   95
    Insurable interest   95
    Valuation   96
    The proposal form   97
    The standard policy   98
    Implied terms   99
    Express terms   101
    Perils of the sea   104
    Exclusion clauses   104
    Third party insurance   106
    Duty to minimise loss   106
    Theft   106
    Making a claim   107
    Total loss   109
    Arbitration   109

10 SALVAGE   111
    Salvor's lien   116
    The salvage award   117
    Salvage agreements   119
    Life salvage   119

11 *HARBOUR LAW* 122
Functions of harbour authorities 123
Powers to regulate activities 124
Provision and maintenance of harbour facilities 127
Harbour authority moorings 128
Harbour dues 129
Light dues 132
Pilotage 132

12 *MARINAS & MOORINGS CONTRACTS* 135
Marina's commission on sale of yacht 136
Access for external workers 137
Work on the yacht within the marina 137
Sub-letting a berth 137
Commercial activities 138
Berth leasing 138
Swinging moorings 140
Rating of moorings 142

13 *GOING FOREIGN* 144
Documentation 144
Flags 145
Insurance 146
Notice of departure 146
Foreign arrival 146
Returning to the UK 146
Rabies 147
Driving licences 147

14 *POLLUTION* 149
Antifouling paints 150
Engine noise 151
Exhaust emissions 151
Sewage treatment 151

15 *TRAILING* 153
General duty to make loads and projections safe 154
Insurance 154
Length restrictions 154
Width restrictions 155
Height restrictions 155
Front and rear overhangs 156
Weights of motor vehicles and trailers 157
Brakes 158

Tyres   159
Suspension, bearings, mudguards and registration plate   159
Lighting   160
Using a boat trailer on the road   162

APPENDICES   163
1 Agreement for the sale of a second-hand yacht   163
2 Agreement for construction of a new craft   170
3 Agreement for the bareboat charter of a pleasure craft   179
4 Agreement for the syndicate ownership of a yacht   187
5 Simple form of salvage agreement 'no cure – no pay'   191
6 Useful addresses   193

INDEX   195

CHAPTER ONE

OWNERSHIP & REGISTRATION
OF A YACHT

The legal principles governing the ownership and management of yachts in the United Kingdom derive partly from legislation, including the Merchant Shipping Acts, and partly from the precedents created by decisions in the civil courts.

The Merchant Shipping Acts, and the innumerable regulations and rules made by the Marine Division of the Department of Transport to amplify those rules, provide a complete code to all aspects of the management of British ships. Although the Acts go back to early Victorian times, modern Merchant Shipping legislation is based on the 1894 Merchant Shipping Act which extends to over 700 sections, consolidating all existing Acts on the subject, and is still in force. However the law does not remain fixed, and since 1894 over 25 amending Acts have been introduced to enable the law to keep up with the changing requirements of both commercial and recreational vessels.

The Acts apply as much to yachts as they do to commercial vessels. The fundamental legal concept is that a ship, although it is not part of the soil of its flag state, and may at any time be on the high seas or in foreign territorial waters, is treated for jurisdictional purposes as being a part of the state whose flag it is entitled to wear.

Requirement to register

Because merchant ships are large, movable, and valuable assets, and because their use or misuse involves potentially immense liabilities to others, it is internationally recognised that every ship should be identifiable through its own national register. International Convention imposes this liability on all states with a seagoing maritime fleet. The 1956 Geneva Convention on the High Seas, to which most maritime states are signatories, provides that every ship shall take the nationality of its owner, shall wear the flag of its owner's state, and shall carry on board documents establishing the link between state, owner and ship as evidence of that ship's right to fly the flag.

So far as British-owned yachts are concerned, the legal position is straightforward. The 1894 Act defines 'ship' as 'every description of vessel which is used in navigation and is not propelled by oars'. Although there may be some argument as to what is meant by 'navigation', the definition applies to any vessel, of whatever size; even a sailing dinghy is included if it is going out into navigable waters, from one place to another.

Obviously the definition does not cover all vessels on every stretch of water. In the case of Southport Corporation v. Morris [1893] 1 QB 359, a three-ton electric launch used on the marine lake at Southport was held, in view of the limited size of the lake, not to be used in navigation. It was therefore not a ship, and was therefore not entitled to the privileges, nor subject to the burdens, of the Merchant Shipping Acts. The later case of Weeks v. Ross [1913] 2 KB 229, concerned a passenger-carrying motor boat used on a canal and river connected by locks to a tidal estuary. The court held that since the waters on which it was used were connected to the sea, the vessel was used 'in navigation'.

The case of Curtis v. Wild [1991] 4 AER 172 involved a Lark dinghy on the Belmont Reservoir. The dinghy hit the crew of another dinghy that had capsized, causing injuries. In the normal course of events the injured party is given three years in which to start legal action for personal injury. More than two years went by before the Plaintiff issued proceedings against the Defendant who then claimed that the special two-year rule that applies to shipping collisions should apply, and that the claim should be struck out. The court held that this particular reservoir (1400 x 600 yards) was not navigable within the ordinary meaning of the word; there was no 'navigation' in the sense of going from A to B for the purpose of discharging people or cargo, and it was simply being used by people for the purpose of 'messing about in boats'. It therefore followed that the dinghies on the reservoir were not being used in navigation, therefore they were not ships, therefore the Defendant could not claim the two-year limitation period, the Plaintiff was entitled to his full three years, and the claim would not be struck out.

Does your water craft fall under the legal definition of the term 'vessel'? In 1992 a court ruled that a Jet-ski was not a vessel recognised under marine law.

A case involving a Jet-ski being used at sea near Brighton Pier was considered in Steedman v. Scofield [1992] 1 LL 163. The Plaintiff was riding a Jet-ski when he was involved in a collision with a speedboat. He was severely injured and brought an action for damages against the owner and driver of the speedboat, issuing the writ more than two years, but less than three years after the incident. The Defendant claimed that the action was time-barred. The court however held that a Jet-ski was not a vessel. In common parlance a vessel was usually a hollow receptacle for carrying people and the word 'vessel' was used to refer to craft larger than rowing boats, including every description of water craft used or capable of being used as a means of transportation on water. Therefore a Jet-ski was not a vessel, and therefore not a ship, and the Plaintiff was entitled to his full three years.

These two recent cases indicate that there is no clear dividing line between what is a vessel and what is not, and what is navigation and what is not. Since the Merchant Shipping Acts apply a comprehensive code of privileges and responsibilities to ships, it will often be a matter of great importance in a legal dispute whether a water craft falls inside or outside the definition.

Owning a ship

Because of the historical importance of shipping to the economy of the United Kingdom, the legal concept of the ownership of a vessel, and the means of recording this for official and legal purposes, has developed differently to the law covering ownership of other objects or 'chattels'.

The legal concept of ownership is best described as the sum total of all the powers of use and disposal of an object as allowed by the law. Ownership of any object, including a yacht, includes the absolute right to sell it, and the right to enjoy quiet and uninterrupted possession of it.

Ownership may be vested in one single individual, in which case he will be treated as sole owner, and his name alone will be on the registration certificate.

Part and joint ownership
If two or more persons buy a yacht together (each joining in the contract with the seller) they will automatically become joint owners of the yacht. They have, between each other, 'unity of title' and no 'distinction of interest'.

An important consequence of joint ownership is the right of survivorship. This means that when one of the joint owners dies, his legal interest in the yacht will pass automatically (and irrespective of the contents of the will) to the surviving joint owners who become trustees of the legal title, for the benefit of the deceased partner's next of kin or other beneficiaries. This means that the deceased's share in the yacht cannot be disposed of without the cooperation of the surviving partners, failing which the executor of the deceased will have to obtain a court order.

Joint ownership may be desirable in the case of a husband and wife team, but is unlikely to suit the purposes of a group of friends owning a boat together. It would be more appropriate for them to be part-owners, each owning a distinct share in the yacht. There is no need for a complex legal document to record the shares owned by such a group; a simple form of agreement for the purpose is reprinted in Appendix 4. As well as providing sufficient evidence of part-ownership, this also deals with the practical aspects of managing an owners' syndicate.

For historic reasons, originally to allow the enormous risks of owning merchant ships to be spread over large syndicates, the British Register of Shipping allowed the ownership of a registered ship to be divided into 64 shares. This arrangement still applies to the Part I Register, and if a yacht in syndicate ownership has the 64 shares allocated between the partners, this will be sufficient evidence of part-ownership and will avoid any of the difficulties caused by joint ownership.

Legal and beneficial ownership

All these principles apply to the 'legal' ownership of the yacht. A person or persons who are legal owners will appear from the ship's papers (and the entry on the Register, if any) as if they were the only persons with an interest in her. They will in fact be the only persons entitled to deal with the yacht, for instance selling her or borrowing money on the security of a mortgage on her. They might however not be the persons who 'own' the yacht in the colloquial sense. Thus for example a large syndicate which may comprise dozens of people who may have contributed towards the purchase and maintenance of a large yacht, and may have appointed a single person who holds the formal legal title on their behalf, or a yacht club may decide to purchase a vessel for club use and will register her in the name of trustees appointed under the club's constitution (in the case of an unincorporated club they must do this, as such a club's property can only effectively be held by trustees).

In these examples the actual owners of the yacht are the beneficial owners, and the persons who hold the title to the yacht are the legal owners. Beneficial and legal ownership does in most cases coincide, but it is important to be aware of, and remember, the distinction.

Registration in the United Kingdom

The registration of British ships derives from Oliver Cromwell's Navigation Acts, the purpose of which was to restrict maritime commerce to British-owned vessels. A later Act of William III provided that only ships entered on the British register should have the benefit of trade between this country and the plantations. That Act described the kind of ship which might be registered, namely ships built in British ports or in certain places in the plantations, and also provided that registration should be granted upon the oath of the master as to tonnage.

The law was amended in the reign of George III to allow for the first time the exemption for small ships of less than 15 tons navigating solely in coastal waters. The 15 ton measurement was a measure of the internal cargo-carrying capacity of the ship without any deductions. A new means of measurement had to be introduced when ships became steam driven to deduct the interior volume taken up by machinery. The present measurement tonnage is based on Simpson's rules introduced in the 19th century, although for craft under 45 feet (13.7 metres) a simplified form of tonnage measurement introduced in 1975 is allowed.

Under British Merchant Shipping law the concept of ownership has always been closely linked with the former requirement that all British ships over 15 tons or used beyond coastal waters should be registered. The effect of this was that any yacht owned by a British subject came within the definition of a British ship, and if he wished to take it beyond coastal waters he was obliged to register it. Although there was no penalty in the UK for failure to register, the consequence was that the owner could have problems while cruising overseas.

The Merchant Shipping Act 1988 changed the emphasis. The requirement to register was repealed, and replaced with an entitlement to register. Also, the classes of persons entitled to register a British ship were widened to include foreigners for the first time, as minority owners.

Formalities of registration

Part I Registration
The British Register of Shipping was extensively overhauled by the 1993 Merchant Shipping Act and Registration of Ships Regulations. Prior to 1993 the Register had been kept by the Registrar of Shipping at over 100 Ports of Registry around the country. This structure was based on the needs of ship owners in the eighteenth century, when it was likely that a ship trading from a particular port would remain attached to that port for a considerable period, and the Registrar, who would normally also be the customs official for the area, would have personal knowledge of the ship and its owner. The list of Ports of Registry reads as a reminder of the great days of British commerce under sail, when such places as Barnstaple, Bridgwater, St Ives and Truro were important trading ports. In 1985 the system was brought partly up to date by the re-grouping of the Ports of Registry into 17 administrative areas, while under the 1993 Merchant Shipping Act all the parts of the Register were centralised and computerised under the control of the Registrar General of Shipping and Seamen based at Cardiff.

Part I Registration is open to any ship belonging to any qualified person including:

- British citizens or persons who are nationals of a member state of the EC and who are *established* in the United Kingdom

('established' is defined as exercising economic activity by means of a stable establishment in the state for an indefinite period)

- Citizens of British Dependent Territories
- British overseas citizens
- British subjects under the 1981 British Nationality Act
- British Overseas Nationals under the 1986 Hong Kong Order
- Bodies Corporate (ie Companies) incorporated in an EC state or having their principal place of business in the UK
- European Economic Interest Groupings registered in the UK

The extension of registration to EC nationals, although in apparent conflict with the terms of the 1956 Convention on the High Seas (which provides that each ship shall take the nationality of its owner), was required as a result of the European Court decision in the Factortame Case (1991-C-246/89). In that case the court considered the provisions of the 1988 Merchant Shipping Act which set up the Register of Fishing Vessels, under which only British owned vessels were entitled to register. A fishing vessel was owned by Spanish nationals who wished to gain the advantage of British registration to fish in UK waters and share in UK fishing quotas who applied for registration but were turned down by the Registrar. On appeal to the European Court it was held that the nationality requirements laid down by the 1988 Act were a breach of the Treaty of Rome which prohibits discrimination between nationals of Member States. In the circumstances the court held that the refusal to register the vessel was unlawful, and the British Government was obliged to amend the Act. This case was important not only for EC nationals established in the United Kingdom, but also created a constitutional landmark as the first instance ever of British domestic legislation being ruled unlawful by an outside authority.

Before registration can be effected, a yacht must be surveyed and measured by a qualified measurer who will issue a certificate specifying the yacht's tonnage and other particulars describing the yacht. Application is then made to the Registrar enclosing the measurement certificate, and evidence of title to the yacht. In the case of a new yacht all that is required is the builder's certificate. In the case of a yacht which is not new, a previous Bill of Sale, or Bills of Sale showing the ownership for at least five years before the making of the application, must be produced. If the yacht was registered on the Part I Register in the previous five years, Bills of Sale evidencing all transfers of ownership during the period since it was registered must be produced.

When applying for registration the applicant should also propose a name by which the yacht is to be identified. The only restrictions on the name are that it should not already be the name of a ship on the Part I Register, similar to such a name, similar to a distress signal, likely to cause offence or embarrassment, have a clear connection with the royal family, or have a port as part of its name if that is not the yacht's 'port of choice'. The requirement for a port of choice derives from the original ports of registry. On the application form the yacht owner must specify one of the 113 ports available. It is difficult to see why the 1993 Merchant Shipping Act did not do away with ports of registry or ports of choice altogether, except perhaps for sentimental reasons. In fact there is no requirement for pleasure yachts on the Part I Register even to mark the port of choice on the stern nor in the case of yachts belonging to one of the former 'registered clubs', to mark the club initials on the stern.

Upon receipt of the application form, with supporting documentation and registration fee, the Registrar will allocate an official number, and issue a marking and carving note. This note acts as an instruction to the owner to carve the main beam with the official number and tonnage. If there is no main beam, a readily accessible permanent part of the yacht must be marked either by cutting in, centre punching, or raised lettering. As an alternative, the number and tonnage may be engraved on a metal, wood or plastic plate and secured to the main beam or other accessible permanent part of the structure with rivets or other permanent fixings. The yacht's name (and port of choice if desired) are to be marked conspicuously on the stern in white, yellow or black letters, contrasting with the background, in letters at least 2 inches high. As an alternative, a carved or engraved block may be attached.

Once the yacht has been properly marked, the owner then signs the marking note and returns it to the Registrar. Unless there is some reason for the refusal of registration, the Registrar then issues a Certificate of Registry to the owner.

The 1993 Act and Regulations, apart from simplifying Part I registration procedures, also introduced a number of new provisions. For the first time, Part I Registration became renewable on a five-year cycle. Before then, registration took effect for the life of the vessel, and the registration particulars remained the official record even if the yacht changed hands, or was re-rigged without the registration being notified. While the requirement to renew the registration on a regular basis places a tiresome administrative burden on yacht owners, it does greatly simplify transfer procedures where the owner of a yacht has neglected to re-register the yacht in his own name and wishes to sell it to another, but is unable to trace the registered owner.

No short-handed seamanship for Olivia Anne IV, *who has her name prominently displayed in accordance with Part I Registration.*

Under the previous rules the Registrar was not empowered to re-register the yacht in the name of the new owner without a Bill of Sale signed by the registered owner. The effect of the 1993 Act and Regulations is that the original registration lapses after five years, following which the new owner will be entitled to make a fresh application for registration. This is more expensive than a simple renewal of registration, but very much less expensive that the application to the High Court that was previously required to change the registered particulars without a Bill of Sale.

Following the 1993 Act, the Registrar may also remove from the Register any ship or yacht that he considers to be in breach of any of the requirements of the Merchant Shipping Act if relevant to its safety, or to any risk of pollution, or to the safety, health and welfare of persons engaged on board the ship. This will operate as an additional penalty for yachts used for commercial purpose such as training or charter work which have not been built, equipped or maintained in accordance with the Codes of Practice. The 1993 Act also provided for more information to be included on the Certificate of Registry in line with the requirements of overseas authorities issuing documents to British ships entering their ports. The information includes, apart from the particulars of the ship and its rig and engines, the name and address of the owners and the name and address of the charterer if relevant, the IMO number, the vessel's radio call sign, the date of issue of the Certificate, and the date of expiry.

A further refinement is that a foreign owned vessel chartered to an entitled person may also be entered on the British Register for up to five years at a time (or for the period of the charter, if less).

Part III Registration for small ships
Although the 1956 High Seas Convention and the 1894 Merchant Shipping Act both imposed strict registration requirements for yachts going overseas, a large number of British owned yachts used to go foreign without complying with the rules. This practice was prevalent particularly in the late 1970s and early 1980s with the growth in small yacht ownership, and the increasing expense of Part I Registration which at the time was the only form of registration available.

In 1980 the French Customs authorities claimed that abuses were occurring, including the wearing of British Red Ensigns by French owned yachts to avoid the payment of French taxes, and the chartering of British yachts in French waters, again without paying tax to the French authorities. The subsequent enforcement of strict registration requirements on all foreign owned yachts entering French waters, copied soon afterwards by the Spanish and Italian authorities, caused the British Department of Transport to review arrangements for the registration of small craft.

The 1983 Merchant Shipping Act introduced an alternative simplified form of registration for ships under 24 metres in length for owners who did not wish to go to the expense of full Part I Registration. Entry on the Register was effected by the simple completion of an application form without any form of supporting documentation. Since the Register was established for the sole purpose of providing documentation for going foreign sufficient to comply with the 1956 High Sea Convention, there was no need for it to act as a title register, nor for any mortgage registration facility to be offered, as with the Part I Register.

Registration on the Small Ships Register was limited to British nationals (and citizens of the Republic of Ireland) ordinarily resident in the United Kingdom, and was valid for a five year period, renewable on application. Following the Factortame case, EC nationals resident in the United Kingdom also became entitled to register their craft on the SSR. From 1983 to 1992 the Register was managed on behalf of the Department of Transport by the Royal Yachting Association; in 1992 responsibility passed to the Driver and Vehicle Licensing Agency at Swansea following one of the Department's periodic re-tendering exercises.

The 1993 Merchant Shipping Act re-constituted the Small Ships Register as the 'Part III Register' (Part II being the Register of Fishing Vessels). Any description of vessel under 24 metres is eligible for registration other than fishing vessels and submersibles, providing it is owned by an entitled person ordinarily resident in the United Kingdom. Entry on the SSR is not available to companies, whether or not based in the United Kingdom.

Entry on the Register is by application form signed by the owner giving:

- A description of the ship
- The overall length of the ship
- The name of the ship
- The name and address of every owner of the ship
- A declaration of eligibility by the owner

On receipt of the application form the Registrar issues the Certificate of Registry without any prior formalities being required. On receipt of the Certificate of Registry (which contains all the information contained in the application form with the exception of the owners' addresses) the registered owner is requested to mark his yacht within one month with the registered number and the prefix SSR on a visible external surface. In practice this is normally done above the rudder stock in an open-cockpit sailing yacht, or on the wheelhouse door or side of the superstructure where appropriate.

Creation and registration of mortgages

In the yacht market a high proportion of purchases are financed by loans from finance houses or bankers. Where a loan is granted to a buyer, even though it may be for the express purpose of buying a particular yacht, the lender obtains no security or interest in the yacht unless the formal documentation specifically provides that security. In the absence of such security the arrangement operates as a personal loan only and the lender can only look to the borrower, and not to subsequent owners of the yacht, for repayment. In most cases where a substantial loan is involved, typically anything over £5000, the lender will insist on taking a formal charge over the yacht. This will enable him not only to look to the borrower personally for repayment, but in the event of the borrower defaulting there will be a right to seize the yacht, even if she has been sold on to an innocent third party, and to sell her to clear the outstanding loan.

The creation of a mortgage gives the lender a prior interest in the yacht which prevents most other creditors selling the yacht in satisfaction of their claims. On the other hand, the yacht remains in the hands of the borrower (the mortgagor) and he retains possession and use of it so long as he complies with the repayment schedule laid down in the mortgage agreement. Thus the mortgage provides the ideal security, allowing the mortgagor continued use of the yacht while protecting the mortgagee's interest in the event of any default.

The protection given to the lender is not complete in all circumstances however. In *The Blitz* [1992] 2 LL 441 the owner of a registered yacht subject to a registered mortgage had failed to pay his harbour dues for a period of time and the yacht was seized by the harbour authority. Although the mortgage was for £10 000 the yacht was sold for only £4000, sufficient to pay the outstanding harbour dues but not the mortgage. The lender took action against the harbour authority for repayment of the sum but the court held that their claim took precedence over that of the lenders. Section 44 of the 1847 Harbours, Docks and Piers Clauses Act empowers harbour authorities to arrest and sell vessels to clear unpaid dues, and the court said that it would be contrary to public policy to allow the owner of a vessel to defeat the purpose of the Act by mortgaging his vessel to another. If that were the case then the harbour authority could have no remedy against the vessel.

A mortgage may be registered or unregistered, according to the status of the yacht. In the case of a yacht on the Part I Register the mortgage must be in the form prescribed by the 1993 Act and Regulations. When the mortgage agreement has been entered into by the parties, the mortgagee immediately has a valid mortgage as against the mortgagor, but until it is registered with the Registrar of Shipping, it will not be valid against any other person obtaining an interest in, or lending on the security of, the yacht. Once the mortgage has been notified to the Registrar on the prescribed form however, the lender's interest becomes fully protected. Where the borrower is a company, the lender must also register the mortgage with the Registrar of Companies as a charge under the Companies Act. Failure to do so within 21 days of the creation of the charge will make the mortgage void against a Liquidator or other creditors.

In the case of a yacht that is either unregistered or registered on the Part III Register, there is no means by which a mortgage can be registered. This does not of course mean that a valid mortgage cannot be created. Most of the major marine finance companies will lend substantial sums of money on the security of unregistered mortgages, on the grounds that to insist on the yacht being registered on the Part I Register can be unduly expensive, and also because the security provided by an unregistered mortgage on an unregistered yacht is as good as a registered mortgage.

In the case of the *Shizelle* [1992] 2 LL 444 the High Court considered the case of a loan by the British Credit Trust. They had lent £40 000 to the first owner to finance the purchase of a 31 foot motor yacht. This loan was made under the terms of a Marine Loan Agreement and a Marine Mortgage, but since the *Shizelle* was not registered, the mortgage could not be registered. The yacht was subsequently sold to the Defendants in the case who had no knowledge of the mortgage. This is always a potential danger in buying a yacht that is not on the Part I Register, as the buyer must rely on the honesty of the seller in disclosing any outstanding charges or mortgages.

Two years after the purchase, the Defendants were notified by British Credit Trust that there was an outstanding mortgage on the yacht. Although they defended the action on the grounds that the mortgage was invalid against them as it had not been registered under the 1894 Merchant Shipping Act, the court held that the mortgage was valid, and that in the case of an unregistered yacht or ship it was not necessary to register a mortgage. Although the court expressed great sympathy for the Defendants, and also stated that the legislature could not have intended to allow unregistered and undiscoverable mortgages of small vessels to be binding on subsequent owners, that was in fact what legislature had done. In the event the British Credit Trust was entitled to sell the yacht in satisfaction of the outstanding loan.

Although it is possible that the law relating to unregistered mortgages may be amended to protect the position of innocent subsequent purchasers, the legislature failed to do so in the opportunity provided by the 1993 Merchant Shipping Act.

CHAPTER TWO

BUYING & SELLING
A SECOND-HAND YACHT

Although the cost involved in buying a yacht, even a relatively modest one, is likely to run into tens of thousands of pounds, and a larger one may well cost as much as a good-sized country estate, the legal aspects can be as simple as buying a piece of furniture.

As we have seen, the Merchant Shipping Acts define a ship as 'any description of vessel not propelled by oars'. Thus any yacht is a ship, down to even a small dinghy or speedboat. By the same token any yacht owned by a British national is a British ship, entitled to registration on one of the two British registers of shipping, and also to all the rights and liabilities attaching to British ships under the Merchant Shipping Acts.

Because of the absence of any compulsory formalities, a yacht may be built, sold and subsequently pass through many hands, from one owner to another, without ever being registered, or without registration particulars (if any) being changed on each change of ownership. This can happen because a yacht is a simple chattel rather than real property (such as a house or land) and because registration is voluntary (unlike a motor vehicle where the Road Traffic Acts require registration, and for every change of ownership to be notified to the Vehicle Licensing Agency).

Although the first owner buying a yacht will normally receive the Builder's Certificate and a receipted invoice from the builder or his agent, in many cases these papers are lost and later buyers will often (against the best legal advice) take over the yacht by a simple verbal agreement with no documentation. This lack of formality does not of course prevent the buyer of a yacht obtaining full legal title to it. However, since the purchase and use of a yacht is full of

potentially expensive problems, it makes sense for the buyer to follow the recommended procedure to reduce the risks to an acceptable minimum.

The contract

A frequent misunderstanding among non-lawyers is that a contract needs to be in writing to be binding on either party to an
agreement. In fact this only applies to contracts for the sale of land
or a house (ie 'real' property) where the Law of Property Act
specifically requires contracts to be in writing. Where the sale of a
yacht is concerned, a simple verbal agreement involving an offer to
buy at a certain price, and an acceptance of that offer, is sufficient
to create a binding agreement.

From the seller's point of view, the quicker and simpler the
arrangement, the better, and it will always be in his interests to
conclude the deal and bank the money as fast as possible. From the
buyer's point of view, however, the consequences of a hastily
agreed contract and immediate transfer of the purchase price could
be (and all too frequently are) disastrous. Unless the buyer can be
certain that the yacht and her fittings are in good condition, that all
VAT and taxes due on the yacht have been paid, that there are no
yard, marina or salvage bills outstanding, that all the equipment to
be sold with the yacht has been agreed and listed, that there are no
outstanding mortgages or legal charges on the yacht, that all the
co-owners (if any) have agreed to the sale, and that the actual ownership of the yacht will not pass to him before he has arranged full
insurance cover, he could be making a very expensive mistake in
parting with his money.

Before entering into a binding agreement, the potential buyer
should be familiar with the terms of the standard form contract for
the purchase of a yacht. Two versions of this are published, one
promoted for use by yacht brokers who are members of the
Association of Brokers and Yacht Agents, the other by the Royal
Yachting Association which is reproduced in Appendix 1. The
buyer should make it clear at the outset, and certainly before
agreeing the price to be paid, that the agreement is subject to the
terms of the standard form agreement.

Parties

Both the vendor and the purchaser need to be sure precisely who
is buying and who is selling the yacht. If the buyer is making the
purchase for tax or other reasons, through a limited company or
some other third party, then that name should be on the contract.
It is also important that any joint owner of the vendor is disclosed,
and the names of all the owners are included as vendors in the
contract.

Purchase price and deposit

While it is customary to pay 10% of the agreed purchase price by way of deposit, the purchaser is free to offer a lesser sum if he so wishes and to amend the contract accordingly. Once the purchase price is agreed, it is binding on both parties unless the survey throws up some previously undisclosed defects, in which case he may be entitled to offer a lower sum. In that case it will be for the vendor to decide whether to accept or reject the lower offer.

Agreement for sale

Where the vendor agrees to sell, by signing the contract he gives a personal guarantee that he has the right to sell the yacht, that there are no other joint owners or other interests that the purchaser should know about, and that the yacht is free of any encumbrances, charges, liens etc. This is referred to in more detail in Clause 7.3 of the contract, and is also enforceable under Section 12 of the Sale of Goods Act 1979.

The yacht and equipment

It sometimes happens that the vendor wishes to retain the name for his next yacht. If the yacht is on the Part I Register (on which every name is required to be unique) the purchaser will have to agree to follow the official procedure to change the name of the yacht after completion of the purchase.

It is important that the purchaser should draw up a complete inventory of all the machinery, equipment and other gear to be sold with the yacht at an early stage in the proceedings. Some vendors who feel they may have accepted too little for the yacht will think nothing of substituting cheap car batteries for the heavy duty batteries that were there in the first place, or replacing some of the more easily portable navigation or safety equipment with a cheaper variety. The inventory forms part of the contract and should be initialled by both parties after a joint inspection.

Value Added Tax and other dues

When a yacht is lying in an overseas harbour, the question of VAT is particularly relevant. Many thousands of yachts belonging to northern European owners were built in the 1970s and 1980s for immediate export to Mediterranean countries. For such yachts no VAT would have been payable in the country of origin, since they were never taken into use there, and none paid in the country of destination since the owner was not a resident and was entitled to make use of the tax-free 'temporary' importation facilities allowed by most countries to encourage tourism. The establishment of the

European Community single fiscal area from 1 January 1993 put an end to such arrangements. From that date any yacht owned by an EC resident, and used in any EC state, became liable to VAT, subject to certain exemptions.

It is important that the VAT status of the yacht (ie whether paid or not, and whether payable or not) is clearly established, and any documentary evidence carefully checked.

Inspection and survey

A comprehensive survey of the yacht is regarded as essential by most purchasers, and the contract is designed to provide a period between signing of the contract and final completion sufficient for the survey to be organised. Usually the purchaser will ask for 21 days to arrange his survey, but where both parties wish to complete the transaction quickly, a surveyor can usually be instructed at short notice and asked to prepare a written report immediately. In practice this need only take 2 or 3 days depending on the availability of an experienced and qualified professional.

It should be noted that all expenses of a survey, including yard fees and preparing the yacht for inspection, are the responsibility of the purchaser.

Notice of defects/acceptance of the yacht

If the surveyor does his job thoroughly, the survey will almost always disclose material defects that had not previously been seen by the purchaser. This will give the purchaser four options:

- to cancel the contract and claim back his deposit
- to propose to the vendor a lower price to reflect the cost of remedying the defects
- to confirm the price but propose that the vendor himself remedies the defects
- to confirm the contract and go ahead to completion

The vendor of course has the right to reject a lower offer or a request for him to remedy the defects, whereupon he is obliged to return the deposit in full, and he is then free to look for another purchaser.

Completion of the sale

If the purchaser agrees to go ahead either at the original price or at a lower agreed price, he is required to pay the balance within seven days of acceptance of the yacht. If the yacht is on the Part I Register, the vendor should hand over the ship's papers at this time. In addition to the Certificate of Registry and Bill of Sale these should include the original Builder's Certificate, the original VAT invoice when the yacht was new, and all contracts and Bills of Sale tracing ownership of the yacht from new to the present time. In practice few vendors are able to produce such full documentation, but a valid Certificate of Registry, Bill of Sale, and proof of VAT payment or exemption should be regarded as essential.

If the yacht is unregistered, or is on the Part III Register (previously the Small Ships Register) proof of VAT payment and a simple Bill of Sale is all that is required.

Vendor's right to assign title

As we have seen, the vendor must guarantee that he has the right to sell the yacht, and that the yacht is free of any mortgage etc.

Free access after completion

A frequent source of additional expense for the purchaser is that a yacht laid up ashore may have easy access at the time of the purchaser's first inspection, but by the time completion takes place may be completely blocked in by other yachts being taken ashore or moved around the yard. Removal of the yacht by the purchaser's contractors can mean great additional expense as yachts are moved around the yard. The provision in the standard form contract provides that any such costs will fall on the vendor, or at the very least the parties are put on notice as to the problem.

Warranties

The exclusion of warranties is an important protection for the vendor, and underlines the importance of a survey particularly when buying a yacht from a private individual. Since the Sale of Goods Act provisions about fitness for purpose and merchantable quality do not apply to private sales, and the vendor is under no obligation to draw the purchaser's attention to defects, the maxim 'caveat emptor' ('Let the buyer beware') should be kept in mind.

If the vendor has made specific claims about the yacht, either by advertising or in written particulars, or even verbally to the purchaser, and those claims turn out to be false, there may be a legal claim for misrepresentation. However, any such claim is likely to be more costly and time consuming than ordering a professional survey which, if properly carried out, will avoid the need for the purchaser to take any notice of statements made by the vendor.

Risk

It is important for obvious reasons that the risk in the yacht should not pass to the purchaser until he has completed his insurance arrangements.

Default

The contract provides for the rights of each party if the other defaults. The purchaser should bear in mind that there is no provision in the contract for a change of heart if he decides that he does not want to buy the yacht after all. Once the contract is signed, and unless the survey discloses previously unseen material defects, the purchaser is bound to proceed with the transaction or risk losing his deposit and any additional costs (including the shortfall in price offered by the next purchaser) involved in a resale.

Arbitration

If a dispute does arise, it is usually preferable to agree to an informal arbitration before instructing solicitors. Legal proceedings should only be entered into as a very last resort after all other avenues of conciliation have been explored.

Entire Agreement Clause

The final clause in the contract stipulates that no other written or verbal statements should be taken into account by either party in interpreting the contract. This does not prevent the purchaser from taking legal action in respect of any misrepresentation by the vendor by which he was persuaded to enter into the contract. A representation does not form part of the contract and thus is not affected by this clause.

The survey

Although a yacht may be in apparently sound condition, the provision in the standard form contract that allows time for a survey should always be invoked. For a cost that is relatively modest as a proportion of the value of the yacht, the survey might disclose such serious defects that the purchaser may wish to back out of the deal altogether, at the very least it is likely to show up lesser defects which will enable the purchaser to adjust the price. The survey will also provide some measure of guarantee of good condition since any failure by the surveyor to find a defect that should have been found will give rise to a legal claim for negligence for which the surveyor will be insured. For this reason it is best to deal only with members of the Yacht Brokers, Designers and Surveyors Association or one of the other professional bodies which require professional indemnity insurance as a condition of membership.

It is also unsafe to rely upon a survey that was carried out for another potential purchaser, or the owner, at a previous date. Although the survey may have been quite recent, and may have shown the yacht to have been in sound condition, if defects have

It is essential to have a survey carried out on any potential purchase, whether second-hand or new. Serious defects, which are not immediately apparent, may be disclosed.

arisen since then, or if the surveyor negligently failed to find certain defects, there is little likelihood of taking successful legal action against him. In the case of the *Morning Watch* [1989] 2 LL 548 it was held that where a survey had been carried out some months before for a different purpose, the surveyor owed no duty of care to a subsequent purchaser who had relied on that survey. The purchaser was therefore unable to sue the surveyor for negligence, and since of course there was no contractual relationship involved, no claim for breach of contract could be made either.

The detailed instructions given to the surveyor are important. It may simply be that a hull condition survey is required, or a full survey to include rig, sails, engine and all other equipment aboard. If the engine or engines form a substantial part of the value of the yacht it is useful to have a separate detailed engineer's report, which may also include a sea trial and full report on the yacht's performance. The surveyor should also be given a copy of the particulars of sale and asked to verify any technical aspects, or references to measurements, that are important to the buyer.

Once the survey and engineer's report (if any) have been received, the contract allows the buyer up to 14 days to decide on his next move. If the survey discloses no material defect, then the buyer is obliged to go ahead with the contract. If there are material defects, then one of the options referred to on page 17 may be invoked.

Whether a defect is material or not can be a frequent source of dispute between the parties. Although there is no precise legal definition as to what is material, it could be said that if the cost of remedying the defect or defects is more than 5% of the agreed value of the yacht, then it is definitely material. Below that it becomes more arguable according to the specific defect concerned.

Lloyd's survey

In former times the majority of larger yachts were built under Lloyd's supervision, and this body still enjoys a worldwide reputation. However in recent years a number of cases have arisen where the buyer of a yacht that has a Lloyd's certificate has found to his cost that it does not provide a full guarantee and financial indemnity against defects. There is no substitute for the buyer instructing his own surveyor and having a report prepared for his own purposes.

Checking the vendor's title

Once the contract has been signed and the survey commissioned, the purchaser should take steps to ensure that the vendor is in a position to pass good title to him upon completion.

For a yacht that is on the Part I Register, the name and port of choice (port of registry prior to the 1993 Merchant Shipping Act) will be marked on the stern, and the official number either carved on the main beam (in the deckhead adjacent to the main mast) of a wooden yacht, or displayed on a plaque on the main bulkhead in the case of a GRP or metal-hulled yacht. The owner should be able to produce the Certificate of Registry naming him as the registered owner. Having satisfied himself that the yacht is the one referred to, including a check on the engine serial number, the purchaser should then contact the Registrar at the Registrar General of Shipping and Seamen at Cardiff (Appendix 6) to request a transcript of the registration particulars. This transcript should confirm the information on the registration certificate, and will also disclose whether any mortgage has been placed on the yacht. There is a need for caution here however since the Register does not allow for the reservation of title, and in theory it is possible for an unscrupulous seller to enter into a mortgage agreement with a finance house (or even to sell the yacht to another buyer) after the buyer's inspection of the register but before completion of the sale, particularly if there is a delay between the events. It is for this reason that buyers of large ships will usually require the transaction to take place in the Registrar's office with the Register open on the table for all parties to see as the money (in banker's draft form) changes hands.

For yachts on the Part III Register (Small Ships Register prior to the 1993 Merchant Shipping Act) there is very little real purpose in checking the registration particulars since the information on that Register is simply an unverified duplicate of the information originally supplied by the applicant. It is for this reason that particular care should be taken to ensure the vendor's bona fides, and the absence of any mortgages. In the case of the *Shizelle* (see page 13) it was held by the High Court that an unregistered mortgage on an unregistered yacht entitles the lender to seize and sell the yacht even if it has passed into the hands of an innocent third party purchasing at a proper price.

Therefore, unless the seller and the yacht are both known to the buyer, he should investigate the title, even if the sale is through a reputable broker, since the broker himself is under no duty to run any checks on the seller's title. Ideally the seller should be able to show documents of title tracing the chain of ownership from the date of building to the present time. These should include the original Builder's Certificate, the original VAT receipted invoice from the builder, and subsequent signed forms of contract and Bills of Sale from the first owner to the second, and so on until the present owner. The seller may also be able to produce a file of recent receipts in his name for mooring charges, harbour dues, insurance premiums, and maintenance and repair work. If these are consistent with what is known about the seller and his yacht, and can be traced back three or more years, then it is reasonable to assume that the yacht is his to sell.

Even if the seller is unable to produce any documentary evidence of his ownership (which is not unusual), he should still be able to refer the purchaser to a yacht club officer, a harbour master, a river or canal authority, or a boatyard. Except in the case of the very smallest craft, such as may be based at home on a trailer, any seller who is unable not only to produce any documentation, or to refer a buyer to someone in authority or in the boating business, should be treated with caution.

Unregistered mortgages

Checking the absence of an unregistered mortgage is a more difficult matter. As the recent case of the *Shizelle* has shown, an unregistered mortgage (assuming the yacht is not on the Part I Register) is valid against the purchaser. Now that a number of leading finance houses lend considerable sums of money on unregistered craft this creates an obvious danger for buyers. An intending purchaser who wishes to be thorough should approach the major marine finance houses to enquire if they have a charge on the particular yacht. Although in theory there is an infinite number of potential lenders, in practice some 95% of the small yacht finance market is probably covered by the five leading marine finance houses, and an approach to them is as much as the reasonably careful purchaser can do to cover himself against this risk.

VAT liabilities

As we have seen, Clause 3.2 of the standard form agreement provides a warranty that any VAT or other taxes have been paid on the yacht.

Value Added Tax was introduced in the United Kingdom in 1972, as a tax on the supply of services, and on the sale or import of goods. Any yacht built in or imported into this country for private use since that date should be VAT-paid and ideally the seller of a yacht should be in a position to provide the buyer with the yacht's original VAT receipt, or at least a copy certified by the builder or original supplier as being a true copy. Unless the seller is able to produce proof that VAT on the yacht has been paid at some time, either in the United Kingdom or elsewhere in the EC, the buyer should be ready to face a potential VAT assessment on the current value of the yacht at any time a Customs official anywhere in the EC carries out a spot check.

Until the end of 1992 it was possible for a yacht built in the UK, for a UK resident, to be exported immediately upon completion without payment of VAT, for use overseas on a tax-free basis. The International Convention on Temporary Importation provided that all convention countries should permit the free use of recreational equipment and 'means of transport' for touristic purposes for a minimum of six months in any one year. This rule was interpreted more liberally than the minimum in most European countries including France, Spain and Italy, and over the years tens of thousands of yachts built for northern European owners enjoyed tax-free status in Mediterranean marinas.

The completion of the single fiscal market on 1 January 1993 saw the end of concessions of this sort between EC states. Following that date, a yacht in any EC state, owned by an EC national for his private use, must be VAT paid. In theory it should make little difference which state the VAT is paid in, since rates are intended to be roughly equivalent. In practice, however, experience has shown that some states tend to be considerably more flexible in agreeing modest valuations with owners, and allowing payments to be spread over an extended period. At the time of writing, the Customs and Excise authorities in the UK are apparently not prepared to discuss valuations or payment terms unless a yacht is actually within the UK (by which time it is obviously too late to negotiate). The importer of a yacht from outside the EC may therefore find it to his advantage to import it first to another EC state where a valuation and payment terms have been agreed in advance (in writing) before bringing it into this country. Once a yacht has been imported into any EC state and VAT paid, in theory no further VAT liability can arise within the EC.

The completion of the single fiscal market on 1 January 1993 also saw the introduction of an amnesty for any yacht in the EC area built on or before 31 December 1984. Therefore if a yacht owner in the EC is able to prove

- either that the yacht is VAT paid or
- that it was built before 31 December 1984 and
- was in EC waters on 31 December 1992 to 1 January 1993

he is not liable to pay VAT on the current value of the yacht. However, those who suspect they may have a potential liability should be aware that there are likely to be spot checks in any EC state on any yacht at any time from 1993 onwards.

The potential VAT liability is something that all intending purchasers should be fully alert to. If the seller of the yacht cannot produce full documentary evidence of non-VAT liability, then arguably the yacht is only worth the asking price net of the VAT element.

A simplified form of proof of non-VAT liability is available in all EC states, known as the 'Single Administrative Document' and issued in the UK by HM Customs and Excise on request to any owner of a UK based yacht who is able to produce sufficient documentary evidence. The inclusion of the document in the ship's papers will considerably simplify things when a yacht is subjected to the inevitable spot checks in the UK and other EC states in the future and in the case of a future sale of the yacht. Details of the SAD and advice on the documentary evidence required can be obtained from HM Customs and Excise.

Formalities on completion

Once the buyer has completed his investigations of title, and has acted on the results of the survey, he will usually wish to go ahead with completion of the sale. Whether this is to be done through a broker or privately, the final balance of the money should not be handed over until the buyer is given the relevant documentation to enable him to re-register the yacht in his own name.

In the case of a Part I Registered yacht, this will consist of the yacht's registration certificate in the seller's name, and a Bill of Sale made out in the name of the buyer and signed by the registered owner. If either of these documents are defective the buyer will not be able to re-register the yacht in his own name, and he will be put to trouble and expense in remedying the problem. If the seller is unable at the last moment to produce the right documentation, then the buyer should consider retaining a part of the price (perhaps 5%–10% of the total) against receipt of the proper documents.

It often happens that the seller did not properly re-register the yacht in his own name when he originally bought it. This does not mean that his beneficial ownership of the craft is in doubt, but it would involve the new buyer having to trace the previous owner (assuming he is still alive and traceable) to persuade him to sign the Bill of Sale in his favour (thus 'leap-frogging' the intermediate owner). If this proves impossible, as is often the case, the buyer will either have to make a formal application to the High Court for an order requiring the Registrar to transfer the title or, following the 1993 Merchant Shipping Act, waiting for the old registration to lapse after the five-year period and making a new application for registration. These problems can be avoided by simple precautions at the time of completion.

Once the buyer has paid his money over, and has the Certificate of Registry and a Bill of Sale in his possession, these should be sent to the Registrar General of Shipping and Seamen with the appropriate fee for change of particulars (£80 in 1993). An amended Certificate of Registry will be returned to the new owner in due course.

For yachts that are unregistered, or on the Part III Register, the procedure is very much simpler since the Register entry and certificate are not evidence of title. On completion of the sale the buyer does not need to obtain any specific documentation, although either the signed contract, a receipt for the money, or a completed Bill of Sale will be useful if kept with the ship's papers and produced as evidence of title when the new owner himself eventually puts the boat up for sale.

Disputes after completion

It often happens that defects come to light after the sale has been completed and the buyer has the opportunity of using the yacht and examining it in greater detail. In those circumstances the remedies available to the purchaser vary from one case to another according to the precise nature of the defect, and whether the seller made any statements about the yacht.

Although the Sale of Goods Act 1979 includes well known implied warranties that the goods sold (even if second-hand) are fit for the purpose and of merchantable quality, these provisions only apply to goods sold in the course of a business, and not to a transaction between two private individuals. However, where the seller makes express statements about the yacht or part of its equipment, he may well be liable if those statements later prove to be false.

In the case of Wills v. Ambler [1954] 1 LL 253, a 4 berth cruiser was advertised for the very low price of £200. The purchaser, inexperienced about boats and interested only in the craft as a houseboat, asked whether it leaked and was told that it did not and that the hull was sound. The vessel was later found to have such extensive rot that repairs would cost over £500. The court held that the representation, although honestly given, was untrue, and that, since it went beyond being simply a statement to encourage the buyer to enter the contract, it should be treated as a warranty. As the craft was, in reality, virtually worthless it was held that the purchaser was entitled to receive his money back.

In the case of Willis v. Claxton [1951] 1 LL 70, the Plaintiff had purchased a speedboat on the basis that the engine had been reconditioned. In fact it had not been, and the buyer could have treated this as a breach of contract entitling him to rescind the contract and to claim his money back. However he chose (as he was entitled) to treat the condition as a mere warranty which was broken, and limited his claim to damages. His award was assessed on the basis of what a complete engine overhaul would have cost, together with damages for loss of use during the time taken to overhaul.

In the more recent case of Sutherland v. Senator Yachts (1988 – unreported), the Plaintiff purchased a Senator 37 intending to use her for skippered charter cruises. Believing the two-year-old ex-demonstrator to be in good condition, he bought the boat unseen, but since the seller was in the business of boat sales, he had the protection of the Sale of Goods Act behind him. Having paid £39 000 he found a number of major faults including an unserviceable generator, a faulty engine cooling system, and a split masthead. Another problem was the boat's range which was advertised as 830 miles at six knots, but turned out to be just 350 miles. This made the boat unsuitable for the Plaintiff's requirements, and he asked the Defendant company to take the boat back. Their response was to claim that he still owed them £2500 for maintenance costs; the boat was arrested in Malta and the Plaintiff and his crew were forced to leave it to go home. The High Court awarded the Plaintiff £115 000, plus costs, when he sued for breach of contract. The award took into account expenses and the loss of potential charter earnings as well as the original price of the boat which, it was held, the Plaintiff was entitled to reject.

Although a purchaser with a well-founded complaint against the vendor may be in a strong position to bring legal proceedings against him, the expense and time involved in doing so, and the very real possibility that the award of damages may drive the vendor into insolvency, makes it unwise for a purchaser to rely on his legal rights. In buying a used yacht there is no substitute for a careful methodical approach using a standard form contract, and a full survey and inspection.

CHAPTER THREE

BUYING A NEW YACHT

Boats built to special order

Unlike the case of the purchase of a used boat, a contract to buy a new yacht, built to the purchaser's order, will invariably be with a professional yard, and all the protective provisions of the Sale of Goods Act will apply. Although it is quite possible to go through the whole process of purchasing and building a yacht without any form of written contract or agreed written specifications, the potential pitfalls for both parties are so great that a detailed written agreement is usually drawn up.

Many boat builders will have their own form of standard agreement, but potential customers should be wary of entering into such agreements without a careful study of the main provisions of such an agreement. If the terms of the builder's own contract are not acceptable, the British Marine Industries Federation publish a standard form contract approved by the Royal Yachting Association. This form provides a reasonable compromise between the requirements of the builder to obtain a deposit and stage payments to fund the building project, and the buyer who needs to have his increasing investment fully protected as the building progresses against the consequences of the builder becoming insolvent. Any purchaser intending to order the construction of a new yacht would be well advised to use the standard form contract. The terms of the contract are set out in Appendix 2, and the principal features discussed below.

In legal terms a boat building contract is a contract for the sale of future goods. In law the sale of goods is not possible at the time

The hull construction is well advanced but what if the builder goes bust?

that the order for construction is given, as the goods do not yet exist, and therefore the passing of the property in goods will normally not occur until the yacht is completed. The parties may however agree to provide for the transfer of the property at an earlier stage, for example on payment of the first instalment of the purchase price, and this provision is included in the BMIF standard form.

Description and inventory

Section 13 of the Sale of Goods Act provides that, where goods are sold by description, any inaccuracy amounting to a 'material misdescription' will give the right to repudiate the contract or to claim damages. This would be of importance where the agreed specification had been changed without notice, or where a particular make and model of the equipment on the yacht had been replaced by an inferior substitute. In such cases, even if the seller is willing and able to rectify the complaint, the buyer is entitled to repudiate the agreement after delivery of the yacht, provided he does so promptly, and provided the complaint is not of a minimal or trivial nature.

Price variation clause

The standard form agreement provides that the builder may increase the price during the building process in line with the

Retail Price Index, provided that the builder has not delayed unreasonably in constructing the craft.

Delivery date and place

Although the time of delivery is of particular interest to the purchaser, the standard form agreement does not provide that time shall be of the essence, and in effect the quoted delivery date is no more than a written estimate of the likely build time. If time runs on beyond the quoted date, the purchaser will not be entitled to claim damages for late delivery under the contract unless he has served a formal written notice on the builder requiring him to complete the construction by a certain date. The notice will only be valid and enforceable if it is realistic in all the circumstances having regard to the stage of construction that has in fact been reached at the time.

Problems of this sort can be avoided by use of the Agreed Damages Clause. Although this is not printed as part of the standard form contract, a suitable wording with explanatory notes is available to be tacked on to the contract and initialled by both parties. As the note to the clause explains, the sum to be paid by way of damages for late delivery must not be a penal sum, but should as far as possible be a genuine pre-estimate of the loss to the purchaser caused by the delay. If the yacht is intended for use for a commercial purpose, then the loss of the estimated net revenue on a weekly basis would be a proper approach; if to be used for the purchaser's private purposes, then the cost of chartering a comparable craft (after deducting the overheads of running the purchaser's own yacht) would be a suitable sum.

Terms of payment

Although it is for the purchaser and builder to come to their own agreement as to stage payments, a normal pricing structure would be for 5%–10% to pass as the deposit on signing of the contract, 30%–35% to pass on completion of the hull, 40% on the completion of the interior joinery, installation of the engine or stepping the mast, and the final 10%–25% on the completion of the acceptance trials and signing of the satisfaction note by the purchaser. Different boats built from different materials will obviously merit consideration of different proportions of stage payments. The intention should be to allow the stage payments to reflect the actual value of the work and materials incorporated into the yacht at each stage.

In the case of a boatyard buying in a completed bare hull, or a small boatyard undertaking a major project that is likely to take up all its manpower and other resources for an extended period, the initial payment and subsequent instalments will usually be required on an immediate basis to provide working capital for the purchase of materials, the payment of the work force, and the cost of other overheads. There is an obvious risk attached to dealing with a yard on this basis. The best boat builders are not always good businessmen and in recessionary times a small yard may be tempted to quote an unrealistically low price for work; in recent years a number of yards have become insolvent through under-pricing their work. Although some protection is given to the purchaser by Clause 11 of the standard form agreement, it would make sense when dealing with a small yard on a large project to take out banker's or accountant's references before handing over a significant sum of money. In addition, the director of a small yard may be invited to give a personal guarantee indemnifying the purchaser against loss in the event of insolvency. There will obviously be reluctance on the part of the yard's directors to give such a guarantee, but if they are keen to have the business, and are satisfied that their company is financially sound, then they should be prepared to provide an indemnity.

Acceptance trial

The standard form agreement provides for the purchaser or his agent to attend an acceptance trial of an agreed length. In the case of a small craft built to a simple specification, this may be no more than an hour or two. At the other end of the scale a large one-off yacht with complex systems to a state of the art design may be subject to days or even weeks of trials in the hands of the purchaser's surveyor. The standard contract provides that if the trial discloses faults, then the builder is obliged to rectify them and provide a further sea-trial in due course.

Once the sea-trial is completed satisfactorily, the purchaser or his agent must sign the satisfaction note, and the final instalment is then payable. Although the standard form contract does not provide for a retention, the purchaser of a complex one-off yacht, where faults or errors of construction or design may not immediately become apparent, may consider insisting on such a provision.

Insurance and termination in event of damages

Since the property in the craft and any materials allocated to the craft are vested in the purchaser, it would normally be the purchaser's responsibility to arrange insurance cover during the building process. In practice however it is more convenient for the builder to do so with one of the specialist yacht insurance companies that provide tailor-made cover for the yacht, materials and component parts. In the event of serious damage occurring to the yacht, the builder has the option either to repair the damage and complete the yacht, or to discontinue and refund any instalments paid to the purchaser.

The standard BMIF agreement gives provision for the prospective purchaser to attend an acceptance trial. The builder is obliged to rectify any faults which are disclosed before a satisfaction note is signed by the buyer.

Passing of property in the craft

Perhaps the most important single provision in the standard form contract is the vesting of the craft, together with any raw materials and components allocated to the craft, to the ownership of the purchaser. This takes effect from the moment the first instalment is paid, even though the sum total for the parts may far exceed the value of the instalments paid. (The builder is of course in turn protected by his lien over the craft until all instalments have been paid.) The advantage to the purchaser of ownership of the yacht is that, in the event of the builder becoming insolvent, the builder's creditors are not able to seize the yacht or any components in satisfaction of their claims, and the purchaser will usually have the option either of having the yacht finished under the direction of the liquidator, or having it taken away and finished elsewhere. For this reason if for no other, purchasers would be wise to insist on the standard form BMIF contract being used. In recent years a number of medium-sized British boat builders have become insolvent, and purchasers with half-built yachts have lost the lot unless protected by a passing of property clause.

Buying from stock

Where it is intended to purchase a series produced yacht, either direct from the builder, or through an agent, the standard form construction agreement is unlikely to be suitable. The terms of contracts offered to buyers vary enormously from one builder to another, and although there is a standard form contract provided by the British Marine Industries Federation, most builders and agents prefer to use their own format.

Most standard form contracts now contain a clause restricting the agreement to the contents of the contract by words to the effect that 'No other agreement, representation, promise, undertaking or understanding of any kind unless expressly confirmed in writing by the company shall add to, vary, or waive any of these terms or conditions'. In most cases this clause will not be objectionable, since it does not invalidate the purchaser's statutory rights under the Sale of Goods Act. However, if a purchase is being made on the strength of promises or statements by a salesman, for example about a yacht's performance under sail or power, or compliance with a river authority's or a foreign country's technical requirements, the purchaser would be wise to insist on any such promises being put in writing. Attached to the statement in writing should be a further statement to the following effect:

'It is expressly agreed between the parties that these additional conditions represent a further agreement as required
under Clause ... of the standard terms and conditions and,
where inconsistent, shall prevail notwithstanding those terms
and conditions.'

The effect of such a clause will be to make the salesman's repre-
sentations, or statements in the brochure, into terms of the contract. In the event that the statement turns out to be untrue, the
purchaser will have an action for breach of contract against the
supplier in addition to the action for misrepresentation.

Payment and passing of property

As we have seen in the section on buying a yacht to special order,
the most serious risk facing the purchaser is the builder becoming
insolvent while in possession of the purchaser's money.

In recent years a number of well-known names in the yachting
industry have gone into receivership, often with considerable
debts, and in some cases purchasers have lost large amounts of
money with no legal remedy. Where a boatyard with a number of
part-built yachts on the site calls a receiver, or has one appointed
by a major creditor, his first act in assessing the value of the stock
and work in progress of the company will be to examine the contracts for yachts under construction to determine who has ownership of the yachts in question.

Where the contract provides that the yacht and all materials
purchased or appropriated for its construction are the property of
the purchaser, then of course the receiver is not entitled to include
those items in the company's statement of assets. An additional
precaution is for the builder to agree to mark all bought-in machinery and equipment with the name of the relevant yacht to enable
easy identification in the case of a receiver being appointed. Of
course if a deposit has only just been paid, and no work has yet
started on the yacht, the deposit will be lost, so it is desirable to
pay by way of initial deposit no more than the purchaser can reasonably afford to lose. However, some contracts for the sale of
stock boats, particularly those imported from overseas, require
payment of 100% of the purchase price before title is obtained, and
in such cases the buyer is at risk of losing the lot. In contrast to the
BMIF standard form agreement, some suppliers provide that 'Until
the company has received full payment for the craft, the property
in the craft shall remain vested in the company', or words to that
effect.

Where the purchase price is divided into a small (5% or less)
initial payment, and a single final payment of the balance on

delivery, this is probably not objectionable. However, where a large down-payment is required (and some suppliers require up to one-third of the total price as a deposit), the purchaser is then at considerable risk until the boat is completed, the final instalment paid, and delivery made. Where a purchaser is asked to sign an agreement of this sort, he would be wise to insist either on the sub-stitution of the BMIF wording referred to above, or the provision by the builder of a banker's guarantee that, in the event of the builder having a receiver or manager appointed, or a petition or resolution to wind up the company, or proposing an arrangement with his creditors, the full amount of all money paid under the contract should immediately be refunded to the purchaser.

If the builder is unwilling to discuss either of these options then the purchaser will have to decide for himself whether to take the risk of putting down a deposit and part payment without any pro-tection. If the builder agrees to amend the passing of property clause, he must also undertake to inform his insurers of the pur-chaser's interest, otherwise his builder's risks policy may be invali-dated.

Be aware that new yachts can develop faults. Here a small racing yacht shows signs of chain plate failure.

Purchasing through an agent

Although most UK yacht builders deal direct with their customers, a number delegate the marketing of their yachts to agents, and certainly most imported series-produced yachts are sold in this way. In practice this arrangement is unlikely to lead to problems, but difficulties have arisen where simple precautions by the purchaser could have prevented considerable losses.

Where, for example, a yacht had been purchased from an agent, and was later found to have a construction defect in the build, the purchaser naturally looked to the agent to cover the cost of rectifying the fault. In the event it was found that the agent was a limited company that had gone into liquidation, and in the absence of any direct contractual obligation the builder refused to take any action. Since no action for breach of contract lay against the builder, the only legal remedy available to the purchaser would have been an action for negligence, which is always more difficult to prove than breach of contract.

Purchasers considering purchasing through an agent should therefore also consider entering into a collateral agreement with the builders to the effect that, should the agent for any reason be unable or unwilling to perform his obligations under the express or implied terms of the main contract, then the builders will accept whatever liability would have attached to the agent.

Other matters in the contract

A frequent source of dispute in the purchase of a new yacht is the specification and equipment to be provided by the builder. Although the builder's demonstration yacht may be fully equipped and fitted with every conceivable optional extra, unless the written contract specifically so provides, the purchaser will probably only be contracting to buy the basic yacht without the extras. The points that need to be clarified, and stated in writing, are whether the yacht is to be the same as the demonstration model in all material respects, whether the engine make and model are to be the same, whether the sails, spars instrumentation and deck fittings are to be the same, and whether the loose equipment will be the same.

A number of builders are now providing a long-term guarantee against osmosis. The guarantee is of course no better than the company offering it, and it may be that if and when osmosis is found, the company no longer exists, but it is still worth asking the builder if he is prepared to offer such a guarantee.

Buying for overseas delivery

Prior to the end of 1992 it was possible for a UK resident to buy a VAT-free new yacht for immediate export overseas, with the Mediterranean coasts of France, Spain, Italy and Greece being the most popular destinations. So long as the owner did not wish to bring the yacht back to the UK at any time, and provided he did not breach any time limit for temporary importation in the host country, he could enjoy use of the yacht on a long-term basis without incurring any VAT liability whatsoever. However, the coming of the Single European Community fiscal area in January 1993 brought the end of this particular VAT concession within the EC.

For an EC resident wishing to base his yacht outside the EC area, it is still possible to avoid payment of VAT, quite legitimately, provided it is not intended to visit EC waters at any time. Thus Turkey, Malta, Tunisia, Gibraltar, or even the Channel Islands, are likely to become even more popular as yacht tax havens, although a Jersey-based yacht belonging to an EC-resident owner may be rather limited in its choice of non-EC cruising destinations.

For owners wishing to base their yachts in other EC states, VAT must now of course be paid. If it is intended to remove a new yacht to another EC state within 2 months of supply, VAT is not payable at the time of supply but will have to be paid in the EC country of destination at the rate applying in that country. VAT rates vary considerably throughout the EC, with some states applying very high luxury rates to larger boats. Buyers should check the current rates carefully before exporting new. The procedure for tax-free removal to another EC state involves the completion and signing of a declaration to certify that the yacht will be removed to another state. The builder will then send a copy of the declaration to HM Customs who will inform the tax authorities in the destination country.

For buyers who prefer to pay VAT in the UK rather than the destination state, this can be done by buying in the ordinary way in the UK, and then delaying export until the yacht no longer qualifies as new under the EC tax rules. This involves keeping the yacht in service in the UK for more than 3 months, and using it under its own power or sail for more than 100 hours.

These rules only apply to yachts over 7.5 metres in length. Smaller yachts must have the applicable VAT paid on them in the country of purchase even if it is intended to export immediately to another EC state.

As we have seen, VAT-free export to a non-EC state is still possible. This necessitates a prior arrangement with the builder and

HM Customs and requires the yacht to be removed from the UK within 7 days of taking delivery. Once a VAT zero-rated yacht has been removed from the UK and it is intended to maintain its VAT-free status, it may not return either to the UK or anywhere else within the EC while under the ownership of an EC resident except by prior arrangement with the local Customs authorities for the purpose of repair or refitting.

The fact that a yacht is being exported does not in any way affect the purchaser's rights under the Sale of Goods Act. Where a breakdown or component failure occurs for which the builder is liable, the owner is entitled to have the repair carried out locally (having first discussed the problem with the builder and given him the opportunity of coming to remedy the fault himself) and to claim compensation for the cost of repairs and any other associated losses. For this reason, any provision in the contract that the builder will only be liable for warranty work being carried out in the UK should be searched out and deleted.

CHAPTER FOUR

CONSTRUCTION & EQUIPMENT REGULATIONS

British Government regulations, imposed by the Board of Trade, have affected the design, construction, equipment, and manning of commercial ships since the last century. However, virtually all statutes and regulations affecting commercial ships make specific exemptions for pleasure craft, or at least pleasure craft under a certain size, with the result that the British yacht owner is probably the least controlled and freest yacht owner in the developed world. In recent years there have been a number of moves, however, to introduce regulations to dictate the design, construction and equipment of pleasure craft, for a variety of unconnected reasons, and it is likely that the limited regulations in effect at the time of writing will continue to widen their net in line with the general increase in regulation and control evident in all aspects of private and commercial activity.

Inland waterways regulations

Although the Thames Commissioners, and their successors the National Rivers Authority, have imposed regulations on powered river craft since the first Thames Launch Byelaws were issued in 1926, most of the other waterways in the United Kingdom have been free of any such rules in the past. This includes the 2000 miles or more of canals and rivers managed by the British Waterways Board, the many miles of Norfolk and Suffolk rivers and the Broads under the control of the Broads Authority, and the numerous lakes and small rivers under the control of trusts such as the

Wey, the Lower and Upper Avon, Windermere, and the Fen rivers.

In 1978 the British Waterways Board introduced regulations for motor craft let out for hire to the public. It was proposed that these regulations, or a version of them, should be extended in due course to all pleasure craft using their waters although it was to be many years before this happened. In 1990 the Board proposed the introduction of new regulations, which proved unacceptable to a number of user bodies. After three years of negotiations, during which it was agreed to promote a joint scheme with the National Rivers Authority and the Broads Authority, an extensive new code of regulations was finally agreed with the main user and trade bodies. It is intended that the rules should provide a common set of design, construction and equipment standards for all managed inland waters, the advantage being that a craft that has been inspected and approved for use on one waterway, can then be taken to another system without having to be re-examined and re-certificated. It is also proposed that local amendments, and grandfather clauses, will be applied to avoid the need for otherwise sound old craft to be scrapped or extensively rebuilt.

The standards have been designed principally with a view to minimising fire risks on all craft except unpowered craft not carrying fuel, or fitted with cooking, heating, refrigeration or lighting appliances. The standards also exempt vessels having a Department of Transport Passenger Certificate, and partially exempt privately owned open craft powered by an outboard engine without any cooking, heating, refrigeration or lighting equipment.

The standards cover the following areas in detail.

Inboard engines

Rules provide for the filling pipes, fuel tanks and fuel feed pipes to be designed and of materials to minimise leakage of fuel or oil into the bilges. This includes a prohibition on the use of glass and plastic fuel sight gauges, and pressure testing of fuel tanks. This section contains a number of exemptions for craft already licensed with the navigation authority at the time the regulations are brought into effect.

Electrical installation and electrically propelled vessels

These rules provide for the fixing and ventilation of batteries, and the installation of cabling of adequate carrying capacity. Also, all electrical devices fitted in any compartment containing petrol or gas need to be ignition protected and an easily accessible master switch to be provided.

Installations of gas, fuel and electrical systems ready for examination by a Standards Inspector.

Outboard and portable engines

These rules provide for the safe storage of fuel tanks, security of the fuel supply system, and proper fixing and silencing of the engine.

Fire prevention and extinguishing equipment

For craft with engines and cooking, heating, refrigeration or lighting equipment, 2 or 3 (depending on vessel length) fire extinguishers of at least 5A/34B ratings must be carried in addition to any remotely operated fire extinguishers which must also be readily accessible. Requirements are also laid down for fire blankets, use of fire-retardant paint in high fire risk areas, and limitations on the use of polystyrene insulation and soft furnishings. The requirement that every vessel should have two means of escape from accommodation areas of at least 0.2 m^2 and 380 mm in width is disapplied to privately owned craft built before August 1993 where it is impracticable to modify the structure.

Liquefied petroleum gas installations

These rules incorporate the British Standards for Installations on Boats Rules which cover pressure testing and pipe sizes and materials, storage of gas containers to ensure that any leakage goes overboard, and provision of proper ventilation and fire protection.

There are also requirements for pipe runs to be kept away from the engine compartment, away from any electrical cables, and above the normal bilge-water level.

Appliances

These rules cover standards for all cooking, refrigeration, heating and lighting appliances. Adequate ventilation of a type which cannot be shut off must be provided, but for seagoing craft there is a provision that ventilators may be weathertight to cater for the worst conditions likely to be encountered by the vessel. In practice the most sensible interpretation of this requirement will be that ventilation can be shut off.

Pollution

No sanitation system capable of discharging sewage overboard may be fitted unless it can be sealed off. An exemption is granted for craft already licensed with the relevant navigation authority.

Boat construction standards

Standards for hire craft, and for new craft built after the coming into effect of the standards, cover the provision of lifebuoys, handrails, openings in the hull, self-draining cockpits, and provision of stop cocks.

Exemptions

Some of the more important exemptions are referred to above. Since the strict application of all the rules would have forced a number of generally sound older boats off the inland waterways altogether, the authorities agreed to a variety of exemptions, in some cases extending to all craft built before the standards were agreed, in other cases limited to craft already registered with the relevant navigation authority. Further exemptions of local effect are expected to be negotiated and brought into effect as the standards are adopted on other canal and river systems.

Application of the standards

So far as waters controlled by the National Rivers Authority (ie Thames, the Fen rivers and the Medway) and the British Waterways Board (ie the canals and the Severn, Trent, and Yorkshire Ouse systems) are concerned, every boat owner will be required to obtain a Certificate of Compliance before a licence registration certificate is issued. Inspections must be carried out at least once every four years, either by a surveyor licensed by one of the authorised bodies (including the Yacht Brokers, Designers and Surveyors Association) or by an inspector who has satisfactorily completed a course run by the British Marine Industries

Federation for inland water craft inspectors.

In the event of a refusal by an inspector to grant a certificate for any waters under the control of the British Waterways Board, the owner has the right to appeal to a Tribunal with appointees drawn from the main user bodies, the marine trade bodies, and British Waterways. The Appeals Tribunal will be empowered to review the inspector's decision in any case and direct that a certificate should be issued.

Department of Transport rules for pleasure craft used commercially

Rules for the design, construction and equipment of seagoing craft, referred to generally as the Load Line Regulations, vary according to the use to which the craft are to be put. Ranging from Class I (passenger ships on long international voyages) to Class XII (pleasure yachts of more than 13.7 metres) the stringency of the regulations is one of the reasons that the majority of the British-owned merchant fleet has now been 'flagged-out' by registration registered in states whose rules are less demanding. One of the outstanding features of the legislation is the wide range of exemptions afforded to pleasure yachts. The International Load Lines Convention of 1966 makes specific reference to the following classes of exemption:

- Ships of war
- New ships of less than 24 metres in length
- Existing ships of less than 150 tons gross
- Pleasure yachts not engaged in trade
- Fishing vessels

For privately owned pleasure yachts under 45 feet, there are effectively no rules. When the rules of the Convention were enacted into British law by the Load Lines Act of 1967, the British Government allowed the following exemptions:

- Ships of war
- Ships solely engaged in fishing
- Pleasure yachts

Between 1967 and 1994 the use to which a pleasure yacht was put did not affect its exempt status. The loss of the sail training brig *Marques* in 1984 led to a review of this policy, and the DTp attempted to apply a new definition to pleasure yachts, arguing that a pleasure yacht engaged in commercial activity cannot be properly called a pleasure yacht. The Department went to the extent of issuing, in 1991, a Code of Practice for yachts used for sail training, although the 1992 High Court decision in the Chalice case (*Times*, 15 May 1991) effectively ruled that the Code of Practice was unenforceable. The High Court ruled that a pleasure yacht retained its identity as such irrespective of the use to which it was put and accordingly remained entitled to all the exemptions afforded to pleasure yachts in the Merchant Shipping Legislation.

As a direct result of the Chalice case, the Department introduced the Merchant Shipping (Vessels in Commercial Use for Sport or Pleasure) Regulations 1993. These regulations provide a redefinition of pleasure craft or pleasure yacht (the terms are used interchangeably throughout the legislation from 1894 onwards) as any vessel which at the time it is being used is: wholly owned by an individual or individuals for the sport or pleasure of the owner or the immediate family or friends of the owner. For company owned yachts, the users must be employees or officers of the company or their immediate family or friends. Any contributions to the owners must be limited to contributions to the direct expenses of the running of the vessel incurred in the voyage or excursion. Where a yacht belongs to a members' club and members all contribute towards the costs, use of the yacht is limited to club members and their immediate family and friends, and any charges made must be paid into club funds.

Thus any yacht used for the purposes of a sailing school, or for bareboat or skippered charter or any similar connected purpose, is excluded from the definition of 'pleasure yacht' and becomes subject to the Load Line Rules unless used less than 3 miles from land and less than 15 miles from the point of departure. Commercially used yachts up to 24 metres in length and carrying fewer than 12 passengers can be exempted from strict compliance with the Load Line Rules if they are certified as complying with the DTp Code of Practice for the Safety of Small Commercial Sailing Vessels, or for the Safety of Small Commercial Motor Vessels.

The Codes of Practice state their primary aim as being to set standards of safety and protection for all on board, and particularly for those who are trainees or passengers. The level of safety they set out to achieve is considered to be up to the current expectations of the general public. The Codes relate to the construction of the vessel, its machinery, equipment and stability, and the correct operation of the vessel so that safety standards are maintained.

The Codes provide that Certificates of Compliance, issued by one of the listed authorised bodies, may be issued for the following areas of operation:

Category 4   Up to 20 miles from a safe haven, in favourable weather and in daylight
Category 3   Up to 20 miles from a safe haven

Even traditional charter yachts now have to comply with commercial craft regulations. They are subject to Load Line Rules unless used less than 3 miles from land and less than 15 miles from the point of departure.

> Category 2   Up to 60 miles from a safe haven
> Category 1   Up to 150 miles from a safe haven
> Category 0   Unrestricted service

Construction and general strength

The Codes require vessels to be weathertight and of sufficient structural strength to withstand the sea and weather conditions likely to be met in the intended area of operations. For vessels built after 1993, a certificate either from one of the Classification Societies such as Lloyd's Register of Shipping or Bureau Veritas, or by one of the Certifying Authorities such as the Royal Yachting Association or the Yacht Brokers, Designers and Surveyors Association, is required. For older yachts, if they are of a design that has at least five years' history of safe operation in the relevant waters, then no special survey will be required.

Watertight bulkheads and damage survival

These requirements apply only to new craft of 15 metres or more in length. Bulkheads must be arranged so that damage which results in the flooding of one compartment will not cause the vessel to sink to a freeboard of less than 75 millimetres at any point. Multihulls over 7.5 metres must be designed to float for at least 12 hours after a capsize.

Stability

New provisions are made about stability of vessels, varying between those with external ballast keels and those without, and allowing a variety of methods for calculating stability for craft under 15 metres.

Weathertight integrity

These rules cover the size and positioning of hatchways, doorways, skylights, windows and ventilators. Ventilators in particular must be provided with a permanently attached means of weathertight closure. Also covered are air pipes, inlet and discharge openings, and the materials for valves and piping.

This part of the regulations makes an interesting contrast to the inland water regulations referred to above which insist that ventilation must not be capable of being shut off. Seagoing commercial craft also used on the wide tidal rivers under control of British Waterways may find it difficult to comply with both regulations.

Water freeing arrangements

These rules cover the size of freeing ports in bulwarks, and self-draining cockpits.

Machinery

In the case of a new yacht the rules require any inboard engine to be diesel powered, except by special arrangement with the Department of Transport. In the case of existing vessels, inboard petrol engines are permitted provided the engine is located in a closed space with an automatic fire extinguishing system, and efficient ventilating systems are fitted, and the petrol tank properly ventilated.

Detailed rules also cover all electrical arrangements, steering and emergency steering gear, bilge pumping, and bilge water alarms.

Equipment

Lifesaving equipment is also covered in detail, as is fire fighting equipment and fire precautions. For craft in categories 2, 3, or 4, a VHF radio transmitter/receiver must be carried. For craft in categories 0 and 1, an MF radio installation is required capable of transmitting and receiving messages to and from land stations, and an EPIRB must be carried.

The regulations also provide detailed regulations for navigation, deck and anchoring equipment, and a full specification for the accommodation arrangements to cover safety and hygiene. These are in part based on the established Offshore Racing Council rules and part on the results of the DTp Working Party deliberations. Other rules relate to personal clothing, medical stores, tenders, storm sails, and deck surface materials.

Manning

For yachts let out for bareboat charter the managers must ensure that the skipper and crew have enough information about the yacht and equipment to handle it safely, and are competent for the intended voyage. For yachts let on skippered charter, the general rules for yachts under 24 metres in length and carrying not more than 12 passengers apply. This provides that for voyages up to 20 miles from a safe haven the skipper should hold a Coastal Skipper Certificate, for voyages up to 150 miles from a safe haven, a Yachtmaster Offshore Certificate, and for unrestricted service a Yachtmaster (Ocean) Certificate.

The rules do not apply to the chartering of sailing or motor craft for use in races under the International Yacht Racing Union or Union International Motonautique rules, and which comply with all the equipment regulations imposed by the organising authority for such races. This exemption does not include sail training races, or any races created to avoid the provisions of the Codes.

Any owner intending to purchase or adapt a boat for any commercial use would be wise to obtain a copy of the relevant Code at an early stage to assess the very considerable costs of compliance.

European Council Directive on Recreational Craft

One of the fundamental objects of the European Community is to encourage free trade between member states. While import duties and other financial tariffs were removed at an early stage in the Community's existence, a number of barriers to free trade still continue. Notable among such barriers are the type-approval requirements imposed by various EC member states on products, for various reasons to do either with safety or conformity for administrative convenience. One such example is the requirement of the UK Government for all radio transmitting apparatus to be tested, assessed and approved by the Radio Regulatory Department of the Department of Trade and Industry.

In France and Italy, type approval requirements have been in place for many years prohibiting the sale in those countries of new yachts unless constructed in conformity with requirements laid down by their governments. In principle the imposition of barriers to trade of this sort would normally be regarded as a breach of the terms of the Treaty of Rome, and action could be taken in the European Court against the governments concerned. However the Treaty does permit member states to implement domestic regulations if necessary for the protection of health or safety, and thus a legal action against France or Italy would have been unlikely to succeed.

The difficulty of dealing with such regulations has meant that few British boat builders have tried to market their products, new, in France or Italy. Compliance with these countries' type approval procedures would have been prohibitively expensive unless the boat builders concerned were proposing to import large numbers of craft. In the context of the boat building market generally, there have been relatively few builders in the world producing craft in large enough numbers to make the exercise worthwhile.

In 1980 an attempt was made by the European Commission, backed by the boat building industry (represented by ICOMIA, the International Council for Marine Industry Associations) to produce a standard set of rules for hull design and construction. The proposal was that all craft produced within the EC area should be built in accordance with a detailed set of design and construction parameters which would supersede the domestic rules imposed in France and Italy. The EC rules were, of necessity, intended to produce strong, rugged hulls that would be capable of withstanding most weather conditions. Since that would have meant a substantial increase in specification for most modern yacht designs, far beyond what was needed by yacht owners, the proposals were eventually scrapped after heavy intervention by the boat users' federations and associations in most European states.

Small Craft Directive
In 1988 the matter was revived, again at the initiative of ICOMIA, in a new attempt to overcome the Italian and French type approval rules. The proposal was for a 'New Approach' Directive using a framework that had been successful in superseding domestic regulations for a number of other consumer products. The planned Directive was to specify a number of component parts of yacht construction, and simply provide that they should comply with the relevant International Standards Organisation (ISO) requirements. The Directive would also make provision for exemptions, design categories, certification procedures, and the marking of 'approved' craft.

The Directive is intended to apply to most recreational craft under 24 metres, including part-built boats, but excluding craft intended solely for racing, canoes, windsurfers and very small craft such as personal water craft (eg Jet-skis). Also exempted are replicas of historic craft, and experimental craft.

The rules will require all member states to establish a system for assessing and certifying all craft placed on the market and put into service to ensure they are not a danger to health or safety. All craft will have to be marked with hull identification numbers according to an EC recognised norm and a builder's plate to be fixed to each boat specifying the area of operation for which the boat was designed, the manufacturer's recommended maximum load and number of persons, and the maximum rated engine power for which the boat was designed. Other requirements will cover visibility from the main steering position, the provision of a comprehensive owner's manual, structural requirements including stability and freeboard, buoyancy and flotation when swamped, openings in the hull and deck, liferaft stowage, escape from fire, and provision for anchoring, mooring and towing. Detailed rules will also cover the engine, fuel, electrical and gas installations, the provision of fire fighting equipment, and the prevention of discharges that may cause pollution.

The precise terms of the final rules are to be decided by the relevant International Standards Organisation working groups. Although the proposals were well advanced at the time of writing, considerable debate was taking place over the potential costs of certification, which could have added up to 10% to the cost of new craft, and potential controls that could be attached to the use of craft subsequent to sale if the information on the builder's plate were to be taken as a means of restricting the free use of craft.

The proposal for a Small Craft Directive, together with a number of other proposals emanating from the European Commission at Brussels for controls on powerboats and sailing craft, led the major user organisations in Europe, including the Royal Yachting Association, the Deutscher Segler Verband, the Federation Française de Voile, and others to form the European Boating Association which now operates to represent the user interest with the European Commission, European Parliament, and the Council of Ministers.

CHAPTER FIVE

CONSUMER PROTECTION

The owner of any private yacht or other small craft who enters into transactions with suppliers, repairers, riggers, sailmakers, insurers, or any one of the many trades and professions associated with yachts, must be constantly aware of his legal rights. These arise not only from common law (ie decided cases in the law reports) but also under a number of Acts of Parliament introduced to give protection to the consumer.

In addition to all this, the yacht owner also has the benefit of a number of standard form contracts for different purposes, designed to provide a fair compromise between the interests of the customer and the interests of the supplier of goods or services. In this context, the Royal Yachting Association has been active in encouraging the use of standard form contracts, and has given its endorsement to a number of these, including contracts for the construction of a new craft (see Chapter 3), for the bareboat charter of a pleasure yacht (see Appendix 3), for the sale of a second-hand yacht (see Chapter 2) and for boatyard terms of business. Any private individual dealing with a member of the British Marine Industries Federation, or a member of an affiliated organisation such as the Association of Brokers and Yacht Agents, can and should insist on doing business on the basis of one of the standard form agreements.

Repair and conversion

The BMIF standard terms of business (11th edition) provides the basis for all work done on yachts by boatyards. One of the most frequent causes of complaints by owners against yards is that the

When dealing with a boatyard, insist on using the BMIF standard form agreement.

cost of the work carried out has gone far beyond the agreed quotation or estimate. Such problems can easily be avoided by the parties agreeing a detailed specification and detailed costs at an early stage. In the case of Hucks v. Hardy [1954] 1 LL 207, the owner had his yacht towed by the repairers to their yard at Hampton Court to slip it, remove the glands, and make good any defective work in the hull having first quoted the charge for carrying out the work. The boat was then left at the yard's moorings for almost two years while the owner contemplated what to do. After that time he was sent a bill for mooring charges at the yard's full rate. The court held that, although some mooring charge was payable, it should not be at the full rate demanded by the yard as there had been no contract for that sum, and therefore they were only entitled to a 'reasonable fee' which was assessed at some 40% below the fee demanded. However, as the owner had simply failed to make up his mind about repairs to the yacht, he was liable to pay reasonable fees for mooring and his claim to be entitled to free mooring was rejected.

In practice, even now, a careless owner will often instruct the yard to carry out work, and to do anything else that comes to light as requiring attention. In such circumstances a yard can hardly be blamed for running up bills greatly in excess of the original estimate. Where a boatyard refuses to give a firm quotation on the grounds that the amount of work to be done will not be known until some dismantling or remedial work has taken place, written instructions should be given that no further work should be carried out without written authority, or alternatively an agreed price ceiling may be applied.

Statutory consumer protection

Apart from the terms of any contract which governs the basic relationship between the consumer and the supplier, a number of statutory provisions have been enacted by Parliament which make the protection of the consumer even more secure.

Position of the supplier

The fundamental rule to remember at all times when making a claim in respect of a defective yacht, or a piece of equipment or gear that has some fault, is that the claim must be made against the actual seller of the item. In many cases the manufacturer may offer a warranty with the goods, but unless he is also the seller, the purchaser's first line of attack should be the trader or company who sold the goods. This is particularly relevant where for example a defective engine makes a new motor yacht inoperable. The builder will often try to palm the purchaser on to the engine supplier, and for practical purposes where a genuine attempt is being made to resolve the problem this will often make sense, but the only party under a direct legal obligation to put matters right is the seller himself.

Sale of Goods Act 1979

The most frequently invoked statutory protection is provided by the Sale of Goods Act 1979 which protects every person who enters into a contract to purchase (or to hire) goods as a consumer. Although the Act runs to 64 sections and covers virtually every legal aspect of the sale of goods that can go wrong, the consumer will be most frequently concerned with Section 12 (Legal right of seller to sell the goods), Section 13 (Goods to correspond with the seller's description or sample) and Section 14 (Goods to be fit for the purpose for which they are required and of merchantable quality).

Section 12 imposes a condition on every contract (whether the seller is a private person or a tradesman) that the seller has the right to sell the goods. If he is not the owner, or a third party has an interest in the goods, the condition imposed by the Act will operate to protect the buyer whether or not the seller knew of his defective title (unless there is an agreement with the buyer to the contrary). Where there is a breach of the implied condition in Section 12, the buyer is entitled to repudiate the contract and claim his money back, as well as receiving damages for any other loss or expense he has incurred. A typical breach of this condition would be where the seller failed to tell the buyer that the yacht was mortgaged to a finance company, or that he was only the part owner of the yacht.

The section also comes into operation where goods have been stolen, but further down the chain of possession change hands honestly. In such cases the thief will usually have made off with the proceeds, leaving the original owner and subsequent purchasers to pick up the pieces. In these circumstances the true owner will usually be able to claim back the goods (since in truth he has always been the owner even though the goods may have been in another's hands), and the most recent buyer will be able to claim back the purchase price, leaving the one who 'bought' the goods from the thief to carry the loss.

Section 13 imposes a condition that, where goods are sold by description, any material misdescription will entitle the purchaser to repudiate the contract, or at least claim damages. This section will be relevant where the specification of a yacht was changed without notice or agreement, or where a specific description in an advertisement was incorrect. Even if the yacht is capable of modification to comply with the original specification or advertisement, the purchaser has the option of repudiating the contract entirely and claiming full repayment of the purchase price.

Section 14 repeats the old legal rule of *caveat emptor* (Let the buyer beware) but imposes on trade/consumer sales a condition that the goods must be of merchantable quality and fit for their purpose. The provision does not apply to goods sold by private persons or through brokers acting for private persons, and thus the buyer of a second-hand yacht which turned out to be in very poor condition would only be able to claim against a private seller if he had misdescribed the condition, or deliberately concealed the defects.

So far as trade sales are concerned, the section defines merchantable quality as being as fit 'for the purpose ... for which goods of that kind are commonly bought as it is reasonable to expect having regard to any description applied to them, the price (if relevant) and all the other relevant circumstances'. The section also provides that where goods are sold in the course of a business and the buyer makes known to the seller, expressly or impliedly, the purpose for which the goods are required, there is an implied condition that the goods will be reasonably fit for that purpose. This provision does not of course apply where the buyer did not, or could not have, relied upon the seller's 'skill and judgment'. The seller is not assumed to guarantee that the goods are absolutely suitable; a yacht or piece of equipment may be reasonably fit for its purpose, particularly when sold second-hand at a realistic price, even though it is known to require repairs.

On the other hand, even a minor defect making the goods unfit, particularly when new, will give the purchaser not only the right to damages, but also the right to reject the goods and reclaim the purchase price provided he acts promptly. For example, some navigation authorities have particularly stringent construction and equipment standards. If, to the knowledge of the seller, a boat is being bought for use on such a navigation with these standards in mind, and it fails to pass the scrutiny of the authority's inspector, then the buyer is entitled to reject the goods unless the defect is really trivial.

If the buyer would prefer to have the defects remedied, then he is of course entitled to claim damages, assessed as the cost of putting the defect right. In practice the buyer and supplier will usually agree that the work should be carried out by the supplier or his agent free of charge; the question of damages will only arise where the supplier refuses to acknowledge his legal liabilities. The question of rejection of the goods will only arise where the purchaser is so disenchanted with the whole transaction that he wishes to take the opportunity of withdrawing completely.

Where a purchaser wishes to reject, it is important that he does so promptly after the delivery of the goods. If there is unreasonable delay, the court will probably decide that the goods have been accepted, despite the defects, or that the purchaser has had sufficient use of the goods to render it inequitable for the supplier to have to take them back. In such a case the purchaser will still have his claim for damages to rely on, although this is less useful as a remedy than the right to reject the goods.

Misrepresentation Act 1967

Historically it has always been possible for a purchaser to take legal action against a seller where he has been induced to enter a transaction by a trick or lie, referred to as a fraudulent misrepresentation. The 1967 Misrepresentation Act gave the right to the purchaser to take proceedings for damages, or repudiation of the contract and return of money paid over, even in the case of an innocent misrepresentation.

A selling agent, including a yacht broker, must be careful not to pass on more information about the goods than that given to him by the owner. If he does so, and the information turns out to be incorrect, the buyer may well be entitled to damages or rescission of the contract (and thus to rejection of the goods) and the broker will be liable to the seller for causing the loss of the sale through his negligence. Any person making statements about goods with a view to selling them must ensure that such statements are not only accurate, but also in no way misleading. For example, to tell a prospective buyer that a yacht has been involved in a minor collision, without also informing him that she later sank as a result of the collision, may well be regarded as a misrepresentation.

So far as the seller is concerned, the only certain way to avoid any risk of an action for misrepresentation on the sale of goods (particularly second-hand goods) is either to say nothing and refuse to answer any questions, or to be frank and give complete answers to every question. Since the liability for misrepresentation applies as much to private sellers as to commercial suppliers, and even a minor lapse of memory about some aspect of, for example, a yacht's service record or performance may amount to a misrepresentation, great care should be taken not only in the writing of advertisements about a yacht, but also in answering questions or making any statements when showing prospective purchasers over the yacht.

From the purchaser's viewpoint, when inspecting a yacht in the presence of the vendor, it is useful to have a second person in attendance who can act as a witness, the more independent the better, as to any relevant statements made by the seller; if the statement or statements later prove to have been untrue, then the purchaser's case for misrepresentation will be that much stronger.

The Supply of Goods and Services Act 1979

The purpose of this Act is to codify the pre-existing common law for the protection of customers receiving goods or services from commercial traders. Thus, although the law protecting customers was not changed by the Act, it is intended to make customers' rights more readily understood. The effect of the Act is to imply terms into every contract for the supply of goods or services (in the same way the Sale of Goods Act does where goods are being sold) about the standard of care and skill to be expected in a contract for services, and about the time to be taken for the performance of the contract.

It is also laid down that the price (if it has not been agreed in advance) may not be more than is reasonable in the circumstances. This will be of particular importance in those many cases involving failure by a boatyard to comply with an estimate of the cost of repairs or alterations to a yacht. Although the Act does not specify exactly what is a fair and reasonable price, this being a question of fact in all the circumstances of each individual case, it does help the customer who feels he has been overcharged. Where an unrealistically low estimate (which is not, in itself, legally binding on the boatyard) has been given, and the final bill turns out to be very

much higher, the customer may well be under a contractual obligation to pay the bill in full, but the Act gives him the right, where
appropriate, to make a legal counter-claim against the boatyard for
their negligence in under-estimating the costs involved. The effect
of this counter-claim may be to wipe out the excess of the final bill
over the original estimate or quotation.

Unfair Contract Terms Act 1977

The main purpose of this Act is to protect the public, and in particular the more vulnerable members, from contractual terms that put
unreasonable requirements on them, or take away reasonable
requirements from the other party.

Prior to the passing of the Act it was possible for a supplier who
had, in whole or part, failed to provide a reasonable standard of
service or goods, to avoid liability simply by relying on the 'small
print' in his standard form contract. This had resulted in a great
many injustices where the aggrieved consumer was held by the
courts to have no legal rights against the supplier because a barely
readable clause on the back of an order form had excluded the
supplier from all liability.

The main provisions of the Act can be summed up as follows:

1 A person (or a company) may not exclude or restrict his liability for any death or personal injury caused by his negligence.
   This applies as much to small print provisions in a standard
   form contract as to the sort of notices previously seen in
   premises (including boatyards, marinas, and yacht clubs) to the
   effect that 'All persons entering these premises do so at their
   own risk, and the management will not be responsible for any
   injury, howsoever caused'. Such signs or contract clauses are
   now invalid, although a statement to the effect that no responsibility will be taken for any injury 'unless caused by the negligence of the management or staff', will be valid.

2 A person (or company) when dealing with a consumer, or when
   dealing on standard written terms of business, cannot, by relying on a term in the contract, protect himself against a legal
   claim if he fails to fulfil the main terms of the contract unless it is
   reasonable for him to do so in all the circumstances of the case.

3 When dealing with a consumer, any attempt by a supplier of
   goods or services to avoid liability to a third party by writing
   into the contract an indemnity by the consumer will be unenforceable, unless it is reasonable in the circumstances.

4 A manufacturer's guarantee for goods supplied for private use
   cannot exclude the liability of the manufacturer or distributor
   for a defect in the goods which has resulted from the manufacturer's negligence.

The sailmaker is probably not liable for defective workmanship in this particular case!

5   The warranties and conditions in a contract for the sale of goods are held to apply equally to contracts for the supply of goods, for example yachts let on charter, equipment hired from suppliers, or goods bought on hire purchase.

Although there is no precise statutory definition as to what may be 'reasonable', the Act provides guidelines to help determine what is reasonable in the circumstances. 'In relation to a contract term the requirement of reasonableness ... is that the term shall have been fair and reasonable … having regard to the circumstances which were, or ought reasonably to have been, known to or in the contemplation of the parties when the contract was made.' The Act sets out guidelines to help determine what is reasonable, in relation to contracts for the supply of goods. These are:

- The relative strength of the bargaining positions of both parties
- Whether the consumer was financially induced to accept the terms in the contract
- Whether the consumer could have got the same contract without restriction from another supplier
- Whether he knew of the relevant term, or might reasonably have been expected to realise it was in the contract
- Whether the goods were manufactured or adapted to his special order

The Act therefore affects the validity of many contract terms and notices used in business and, so far as boat owners are concerned, provides a reasonable level of protection against carelessness in reading the small print.

Consumer Credit Act 1974

The main purpose of this Act is to provide a strict code of conduct for financial companies and other suppliers of consumer credit. Failure to comply with the statutory requirements, particularly as to quoting accurate interest rates, the giving of full information, providing 'cooling-off' periods for loan agreements entered into at the customer's home, and the exact format that written loan agreements are to take can result in financial penalties for lenders, and make a loan agreement unenforceable. The Act also provides for extortionate credit agreements to be rectified, and a lower rate of interest to be ordered by the court.

So far as the average boat owner is concerned, perhaps the most important provision in the Act is the extension of the supplier's liabilities to the creditor in the case of debtor/creditor/supplier agreements. In effect this means (in the case of any transaction below £15 000) that a failure by the supplier to honour his obligations either under the contract or the Sale of Goods Act or any other legislation will create a similar obligation on the part of the creditor. Thus a boat owner buying defective equipment for his yacht by credit card, or through a personal loan agreement where the creditor pays the money direct to the supplier, who subsequently fails to obtain satisfaction from the supplier for the defective goods, has a legal claim against the bank or finance house which provided the credit.

Consumer Protection Act 1987

This Act gives effect in the United Kingdom to the European 'Product Liability Directive', in order to harmonise European law on the manufacturer's ultimate liability to victims of defective products. The effect of the Act is that any person who produces, or imports into the European Community area, any product, is liable for any damage caused wholly or partly by a defect in the product. A product is defined as being defective if the safety of the product is not such as persons generally are entitled to expect, and damage to other property, as well as death or personal injury, is covered by the Act.

Section 5(2) of the Act provides that damage to the product itself is not covered. There must be consequential damage to other property or to persons. Where property is damaged, the Act will only apply where it is of a sort intended for private use, occupation, or consumption, and actually intended by the person suffering the loss or damage mainly for his own private use or occupation, and the damage must be in excess of £275 for liability to arise.

As well as creating civil liability, the Act also imposes criminal liability on any person who supplies consumer goods which fail to comply with the general safety requirement. The Act also extends the normal time limitation period of six years, by allowing a Plaintiff to take legal action any time up to ten years after the cause of action has arisen.

The overall effect of the Act is to put the injured party in a stronger legal position. Prior to the Act, an aggrieved purchaser of defective equipment which caused damage could only bring an action against the supplier (not the manufacturer) under the contract, or against the manufacturer if there was evidence of negligence on his part. The position now is that the manufacturer has direct liability to the ultimate consumer without negligence having to be proved against him.

Trade Description Act 1968

The purpose of this Act is to provide criminal sanctions against traders giving false or misleading trade descriptions in relation to goods, and is administered generally by the local authorities. Any person in the course of a trade or business could be liable, but the two defences of reasonable diligence, and having taken due precautions not to publish misleading statements, are intended to ensure that only cases where traders have acted intentionally or recklessly should be prosecuted.

The definition of 'trade description' is very wide, and includes statements as to methods of manufacture, fitness for purpose, strength, performance, behaviour, or accuracy. Thus if a chandler is asked if a rope will withstand a certain load, his answer must be accurate, although his liability will be criminal and will not give the buyer any right to damages in the civil courts. Of course the buyer will still have his rights under the Sale of Goods Act and the Misrepresentation Act.

The Act also applies to the trade publisher of misleading advertisements unless he can show that he did not know, and had no reason to suspect, that the publication of a particular advertisement would amount to an offence. It is also an offence for any person in the course of any trade or business to make a statement which he knows to be false; or recklessly to make a statement which is false, as to the provision or nature of any services, accommodation, or facilities, or as to the time at or manner in which these may be available.

Taking legal proceedings

Despite all the precautions a boat owner may take in using a reputable member of the trade, in carefully examining the terms of the proposed contract, and in keeping a positive dialogue going with the trader (be he a boat builder, boatyard, or other supplier of goods or services) disputes will inevitably arise which good will and negotiation cannot resolve. In such circumstances the boat owner has a number of decisions to make, including whether to handle the claim himself, whether to appoint a surveyor or solicitor (or both), and whether to take the matter to private arbitration or to the County (or High) Court.

Solicitor or surveyor?
It will often happen, particularly where the dispute arises as to the standard of work, the price paid, or some other relevant term of the contract, that the customer's chances of success in a legal action depend very much upon the evidence of expert witnesses, and the overall impression that they make on the judge or arbitrator if the matter eventually comes to court.

The conventional approach to legal proceedings is for the aggrieved party to engage a solicitor who will attempt to negotiate with the other party, failing which he will then instruct a surveyor to examine the evidence, prepare a written report, and eventually appear in court as the customer's expert witness. Experience has shown, in many cases, that this is neither the most economical approach nor the procedure most likely to succeed, for a number of reasons.

Where a dispute arises, and cannot be resolved by direct negotiation between the parties, it is likely that both sides have a valid case to make, but that strong personal differences have arisen which make it likely that the matter will end in court. The appointment of a solicitor by the customer will inevitably aggravate the personal differences between the two sides, since it will inevitably be seen as a declaration of legal hostilities. Moreover, unless the customer has taken steps to find the right solicitor for the job (and there are relatively few in the country who are familiar with this branch of the law) it is possible he will instruct one who will rapidly find himself out of his depth, adding unnecessary extra cost to the proceedings, and prejudicing the chances of a swift and satisfactory outcome.

The appointment of an experienced surveyor as a first step however has a number of potential advantages. In the first place, the surveyor will be able to assess the case as a whole and advise the customer whether the work or goods are satisfactory. He will be able to advise whether he has been overcharged or whether he has been fairly dealt with and should drop the case. Having advised his client on the strength of his case he will then be able to approach the supplier as an intermediary rather than in the combative spirit adopted by some solicitors. The fact that he is an expert, and respected in his field, will often influence the supplier sufficiently to review his own position and made a satisfactory offer of settlement.

Only if the surveyor's initial approach to the supplier fails, and it becomes clear that legal proceedings are inevitable, should a solicitor be appointed. This again is a matter that the surveyor can advise on to ensure that the right firm and the right lawyer is instructed for the job. The fact that the firm is instructed later than would conventionally be the case will in no way prejudice the outcome of the case, since the surveyor will in any event be the central player in subsequent legal proceedings as an expert witness, and the costs of the unsuccessful attempt at settlement will probably be very much less if conducted by a surveyor than a solicitor.

In most cases therefore there is much to gain and little to lose in appointing a surveyor before the solicitor.

There are certain cases, however, where legal action cannot be delayed, or where the case depends on the legal interpretation to be given to a contract or a statute, when the question of expert evidence does not arise, and a solicitor should be appointed immediately. However, such cases are unusual; in most cases it is likely that the approach outlined above will be the best.

Arbitration or legal action?
It often happens that a dispute cannot be resolved either by negotiation between the parties, or through their surveyors or legal

advisers, in which case the customer will have to decide, if he is
determined to seek redress, to take the matter either to arbitration or to the courts.

If the sum total of the claim is £50 000 or less, then proceedings
may be initiated in the County Court within whose jurisdiction
the Defendant resides or carries on business, or where the original contract was agreed or the cause of action arose. Since County
Court proceedings are generally speedier, simpler and cheaper
than High Court proceedings it will often be worthwhile trim-
ming down the amount of a claim to a sum not exceeding £50 000
to stay within the limit of jurisdiction.

However, most standard forms of contract provide that any
dispute arising between the parties will be submitted to an independent arbitrator chosen by the parties, or if they cannot agree
on a nomination, to be chosen by the BMIF or RYA or one of the
professional institutions. The advantage of a private arbitration is
that the arbitrator will normally have a good expert knowledge
of the problem under dispute, proceedings can be much faster
and less formal, and there is rarely any need to employ professional legal advisers, although an arbitrator may well agree to
hear evidence from a surveyor if one has been instructed by
either of the parties.

The disadvantage is that the arbitrator will not have the same
legal background as a judge, and will usually tend to look for a
compromise solution rather than coming down firmly on one
side or the other. Also, if either of the parties is dissatisfied with
the arbitrator's decision, there is no appeal unless he has clearly
misapplied the law. Furthermore, if the arbitrator's decision is
subsequently ignored by the unsuccessful party, the only way in
which it can be enforced is by taking legal action through the
courts, so arbitration should only be embarked upon if the customer is satisfied that the supplier is likely to abide by the arbitrator's decision.

As a general rule a dispute involving questions of fact may be
safely left to an arbitrator to decide; questions of law and legal
construction of contracts are not suitable for a non-legally qualified person, and should be taken to court.

Award of damages

The Plaintiff in a legal action for breach of contract or misrepresentation may be claiming damages alone, or damages with
rescission of the contract and return of the purchase price, or
damages coupled with some other order of the court. Careful
thought must be given to the exact amount of damages that
should be claimed. The principle governing an award of damages
is that the successful Plaintiff should so far as possible be com-

pensated for all losses arising from the Defendant's breach of contract. He should, as far as money can do it, be placed in the same position as if the contract had been fully performed. In assessing damages the court will only take account of the strict legal obligations of the unsuccessful Defendant, and of course if the Plaintiff cannot prove an actual monetary loss then he will only be entitled to nominal damages.

CHAPTER SIX

RULES OF THE ROAD
& COLLISIONS

Although there are many legal requirements and regulations that apply to private pleasure craft, the United Kingdom remains one of the few states in the developed world where a private owner can take his craft to sea without compulsory licensing, registration or third party insurance, and without having to comply with compulsory construction and equipment regulations. By contrast, commercial shipping in the UK is subject to such stringent conditions covering every aspect of the vessel and its use that literally thousands of British owned ships are now 'flagged-out' by being registered in less demanding states.

The reason for this apparent inconsistency is that the present shipping rules in the UK were developed in the 18th and 19th centuries by a Board of Trade that recognised the distinction between profit-led commercial shipping where there was every incentive for owners to cut corners, and privately owned yachts where the owners' personal pride would ensure that the vessel was built, maintained and crewed to the highest standard. By definition those owners were the rich and titled in society, but the distinction between commercial use and private use remains as valid today as ever.

One set of rules that applies equally to all craft on navigable waters however is the International Regulations for Preventing Collisions at Sea, 1972. These rules are given international effect as part of the Final Act of the International Conference on Safety of Life at Sea, 1960, Annex B. The rules form a codification of centuries of maritime practice between seamen to keep ships clear of each other. Established originally by custom and practice, the rules were first codified by Trinity House in 1840, but it was not

According to the prevention of collision regulations, 'A vessel of less than 20 metres in length or a sailing vessel shall not impede the passage of a vessel which can safely navigate only within a narrow channel or fairway'. There's little doubt who would be the winner in a duel with an Isle of Wight ferry!

until the Brussels Convention of 1910 was agreed that an internationally recognised code came into effect, eventually forming the basis of the 1960 code, which itself was updated by the Conference of 1972 sponsored by the International Maritime Organisation, and again in 1981. Ninety-five of the world's states have signed the Convention, representing over 96% of the world's tonnage. The current Collision Regulations are enacted into English law by the Merchant Shipping (Distress Signals and Prevention of Collision) Regulations 1983, and Section 418 of the Merchant Shipping Act 1984. The Act provides criminal penalties for breaches of the collision regulations; so far as civil liability for damage is concerned, breach of the collision regulations, leading to damages, is an essential element in proving negligent navigation.

Collision between vessels may happen anywhere in British or foreign territorial waters or on the high seas. Vessels of different nationalities may be involved, and the first question to be settled in any such case is where the legal action should be heard. The English Admiralty Court exercises a wide jurisdiction in all maritime cases, and foreign litigants will often choose to take cases to the English courts for resolution under English law. The English legal system has a good reputation, as Lord Denning has said, 'for the quality of the goods and the speed of service'. In the 1984 case of *The Abidan Diver* [1984] AC 398, a collision occurred between a Turkish and a Cuban vessel in the Bosporus. The Turkish ship owners arrested the Cuban vessel and started a collision action in the Turkish court. Three months later the Cuban ship owners arrested, in England, a sister ship (ie a ship in the same ownership) of the Turkish vessel and started an action in the Admiralty Court. When the Turkish ship owner applied to stay the action in England, the Admiralty Court had to decide the application on the basis of which of the two courts was the most convenient to the parties. Both accepted that the case had no connection whatever with England, but the Turkish party still had to prove the Turkish courts were equal in every way to the European courts, that it was more convenient for the Turks to have the case heard there, and that it was no less convenient for the Cubans. Having demonstrated all those matters to the satisfaction of the court, the Turks succeeded in having the English proceedings stayed.

In practice, the choice of court by the Plaintiff will be based on his assessment of his own (and his witnesses') convenience, whether the legal system of the country will provide an adequate remedy, and whether the Defendant has any assets within that country or accessible (eg by reciprocal judgment enforcement treaties) from that country.

The legal principle is that any country may entertain actions for unlawful acts committed in its territory, and since ships are in a sense part of that territory, the offending vessel can be said to have committed the act on that nation's territory.

When a collision occurs, the vessels involved are bound to exchange the names of the craft and where registered, as well as the names of their home ports, and the ports from which they have come and to which they are proceeding. They also have a duty, imposed in the United Kingdom by Section 422 of the Merchant Shipping Act 1894, to stand by and render any assistance to each other, provided they can do so without unreasonably adding to their own danger. This is in addition to the general duty under the Maritime Conventions Act 1911 (Section 6) to render assistance to any person in danger at sea.

A collision between two vessels usually involves the legal tort of negligence, that is, an unlawful act (or omission) on the part of someone who owes a duty of care to the injured party. Just as damages will usually be payable in the case of a collision between cars, so the same principle applies to ships. Although the procedural rules in the Admiralty Court are very different to the other courts, the principles of negligence remain the same, and if the Plaintiff can prove that the other party showed 'a want that attention and vigilance which is due to the security of other vessels that are navigating the same seas' he is likely to win his case.

When a case comes to court for adjudication, it will not be decided according to any uniquely legal principles, but in accordance with the facts of the case as they appear in the light of common sense. Negligence charged in collision cases may not necessarily mean negligent boat handling. It may also be negligence in the management or equipping of the yacht. Failure to care adequately for equipment, a breakdown of steering gear due to neglect or carelessness, or the parting of an inadequate mooring rope, could amount to an actionable fault. A successful defence to such an allegation could be that the defect was latent – ie not discoverable even by the exercise of due diligence, so that the yacht had been taken to sea in as efficient and safe condition as the exercise of reasonable care could ensure.

Special position of racing yachts

Where a collision occurs between two racing yachts, although the International Yacht Racing Rules will be relevant in assessing liability, the provisions of the Collision Regulations will be the determining factor in deciding liability. Some aspects of damage between racing yachts are examined below, but two rules are of particular relevance in the immediate aftermath of a racing collision.

Fundamental Rule D requires a yacht which has infringed a right of way rule to retire (or take an alternative penalty) immediately. Because insurers are very sensitive about admissions of liability, some owners fear that an immediate retirement might be construed as an admission of liability for damage caused to the other yacht, which might give their insurers grounds for rejecting the claim. In fact this is not the case; an act or error of judgment that may be an infringement of the racing rules will not necessarily amount to negligence for the purposes of civil law. In any event it would be quite wrong for an insurer to reject a claim for this reason; the insurer covers the yacht for racing risks, and the cover implies that the insurer has knowledge of, and accepts, the precise terms of all the racing rules, including the obligation to retire promptly. Thus the duty on the offending yacht to retire prevails over the requirement of the insured not to take any action that may amount to an admission of liability.

A frequent cause of many unnecessary protests is the belief by the owner of a damaged yacht that, unless he can win a protest about the incident, he will not be able to claim damages later in the courts. This again is entirely without foundation. The Royal Yachting Association prescription to Rule 76.1 (which allows individual national authorities to make their own rules on the point) provides that the findings of fact of a protest committee can only be brought into evidence in a civil court with the written consent of both parties; in other words such findings are irrele- vant to the question of liability for damage.

The owner of a damaged yacht who takes protest proceedings would be wise, in addition, to take a separate signed statement, preferably on the same day, from any useful witnesses who are called to the protest. If there are to be court proceedings as a result of the collision, they will probably be at least a year later, and time can play tricks on a witness's memory. A contempora- neous written statement of all the relevant facts seen by an inde- pendent witness can prove to be a useful asset in due course.

Proving fault

As we have seen, the questions of good and prudent seamanship are questions of fact, not of law. The burden of proving that a col- lision arose from another's negligence lies on the party asserting negligence; it is for him to prove both the breach of duty of good seamanship, and that the damage suffered was a direct conse- quence of that breach of duty. This may or may not involve a breach of the Collision Regulations, but it is obvious that proof of a breach of the Regulations will be the best possible evidence of negligence, particularly where one of the vessels is in breach of one of the defined situations such as the crossing or overtaking rules.

Defences

In practice very few collisions are so straightforward that a court will find wholly in favour of one of the parties, and there are a number of defences that a party can call on to avoid being held fully responsible for the damage.

A Defendant may try to rely on the defence of inevitable acci- dent. This is available as a defence if it can be shown that the proximate cause of the accident was some external event beyond the ship's control and not to be avoided by ordinary skill and care or common foresight. An example of this might be the sud- den breaking of steering gear, or a sudden and unexpected squall. In a recent County Court case a motor yacht was manoeuvring slowly in a marina when the remote gear change apparatus stuck in the ahead position. The Defendant was able to show that he took reasonable care to have his installation serviced on a regular basis. His expert surveyor who investigated the accident was unable to determine the cause of the fault, and could only recreate the fault by removing the gearbox cover and 'helping' the cable to jump its guide. The court took the view that this was a million-to-one chance from which no liability arose.

The fact that a collision is caused by a mechanical failure will only be a defence if the failure arose through no fault of the Defendant. In the case of *The Merchant Prince* [1892] P 179 a collision occurred as a result of the steering wheel becoming jammed. The probable cause of the jamming was that the chain connecting the steering gear with the rudder had been allowed to become loose, causing kinks in the linkage. The court held that the Defendant had been negligent in maintaining the steering gear, and was thus liable.

Admiralty law differs from the normal legal principles in the allocation of costs after a successful defence of inevitable accident. Normally the successful Defendant would be entitled to have his legal costs paid by the Plaintiff, if the Plaintiff's claim has been dismissed. The Admiralty Courts however have a different rule. Proof of negligence is particularly difficult in marine cases, and even less than elsewhere can the outcome of a collision case be forecast. The Admiralty Court has therefore developed the practice that where it dismisses an action on the ground of inevitable accident, each party pays its own costs, and the unsuccessful Plaintiff is not saddled with those of the Defendant. But if it should have been obvious that it was an inevitable accident which caused the collision, the court will dismiss the action with costs.

Contributory negligence

The difficulty of proving absolute fault on either side is reflected in the high proportion of cases which are decided on an apportionment of blame. Historically, the rule in the Admiralty Court was that where both parties were partly to blame, each was required to carry half of the total loss. This was a crude approach which could result in an injustice to one of the parties, particularly if the one whose negligence was comparatively slight, also suffered much less than the other. In such a case he would have to make a substantial payment to the other. This rule was changed by the International Collision Convention, 1910, which was incorporated into British law by Section 1 of the Maritime

Conventions Act 1911. This provides:

> 'Where, by the fault of two or more vessels, damage or loss
> is caused to one or more of those vessels, to their cargoes or
> freight, or to any property on board, the liability to make
> good the damage or loss shall be in proportion to the degree
> in which each vessel was in fault.'

Under these circumstances there is an infinitely variable potential
for apportioning liability, particularly where three or more vessels may have been involved in an incident (which is a common
occurrence in yacht racing fleets).

In the case of the *Kylix* and the *Rustringer* [1979] 1 LL 133 the
Kylix had been held to have kept a bad lookout, attempted to
overtake too closely, and failed to give an overtaking signal or
prior agreement by radio as required in the local byelaws. The
Rustringer was also held to have kept a bad lookout, altered
course to starboard at an improper time without signalling, and
failed to keep to port as required by the byelaws. However the
main responsibility for overtaking safely was on the *Kylix* and
liability was apportioned 80%/20%.

In the *Miraflores* and *Abadesa* [1967] 1 LL 191, a case which was
decided in the House of Lords, the vessel *Liranos* went aground
as a result of taking evasive action when the ships *Miraflores* and
Abadesa collided in the River Scheldt. The *Miraflores* and *Liranos*
were inbound to Antwerp. The *Abadesa*, a small coaster, had
steered violently across their path when caught in a cross current.
The *Miraflores* reduced speed, as did the *Liranos* half a mile
astern. The cross current then caught the *Miraflores* which collided with the *Abadesa*, spilling oil which caught fire. In attempting to avoid the area, the *Liranos* ran aground, requiring 10 tugs
to refloat her.

The *Liranos* claimed against the *Miraflores* and *Abadesa*; and the
Miraflores and the *Abadesa* claimed against each other. The House
of Lords, on appeal from the Admiralty Court and the Court of
Appeal, held that, the *Liranos* was 40% to blame so far as the
damage to the *Liranos* was concerned, the *Miraflores* 20%, and the
Abadesa 40%.

Similar principles are applied in assessing liability between
yachts colliding, whether in the course of a race or not. It will
often happen that the insurers of the two or more yachts concerned, rather than taking expensive and protracted legal proceedings, will agree to be bound by the findings of a privately
appointed arbitrator who will determine liability on the basis of
written statements by the parties and independent witnesses.

The court will not always find it necessary to apportion liability, particularly in cases where one party has been seriously

negligent. An incident involving a racing yacht in collision with a commercial vessel resulted in a finding of full liability against the racing yacht. In the case of the *Glucometer II* [1989] 1 LL 54 a racing catamaran competing in the 1985 City of Plymouth Round Britain Race collided with a ship in thick fog 4 miles south of Beachy Head. The race instructions provided that all competitors should carry a radar reflector on board, but left it to the discretion of the crews as to when this should be hoisted in the rigging. The crew of the yacht had a proper radar reflector aboard, but were relying on a home made apparatus (aluminium foil inside a stocking inside the mast) on the day in question. The yacht was not visible to the ship's radar and a collision ensued. The court held that to sail in thick fog with no proper radar reflector amounted to seriously negligent navigation and accordingly the yacht owner's claim failed. In addition he had to pay for damage inflicted on the ship.

There are also circumstances in which the court may find that neither party has been negligent in the course of a yacht race, where similar circumstances involving vessels not racing would be clear evidence of negligence. This arises from the different philosophy underlying the Racing Rules and the Collision Regulations; while the Racing Rules are intended to govern the actions of yachts manoeuvring in very close proximity to each other and indeed encouraging them to do so, the Collision

In the course of a race, a helmsman will have to make snap decisions where an error of judgment may have serious consequences.

Regulations are intended to keep vessels as far as possible away from each other. While negligence in either case will depend on the Plaintiff being able to prove a lack of seamanlike behaviour on the part of the Defendant, it is inevitable that in racing collisions there will be many more grey areas where the Defendant will be given the benefit of the doubt. In the course of a race a helmsman will have to make snap decisions where an error of judgment may have serious consequences.

In an unreported County Court case involving two Lasers running in close pursuit at the Hillingdon Sailing Base, the leading Laser capsized and the helmsman of the following Laser took inadequate avoiding action, damaging the capsized craft. The court held that this error of judgment by the following craft did not amount to negligence (even though he was in the wrong under the IYR Rules and retired promptly after the collision).

Circumstances may also arise where a yacht that is in the right under the Racing Rules may be held liable for civil damages following a collision. The right of way yacht may well be entitled to strike another yacht while racing (subject to disqualification under Rule 32 only if the damage is serious enough to cause the damaged yacht to retire) but if the collision could easily have been avoided, or if indeed it was intentional, may be liable to pay for the other's repairs. Such circumstances may arise at a crowded turning mark where a yacht entitled to claim room at the mark forces a passage knowing that it is likely to cause damage, and chooses to hit the other yacht rather than go behind her. Similarly, in handicap fleets where yachts of different size, speed potentials, and manoeuvring ability are involved, a small, handy right of way yacht will almost inevitably have a legal liability to avoid collisions with a slower and heavier yacht even though she may have the right of way at the time.

Principles of compensation

The purpose of the award of damages by a court is to place the owner of the damaged vessel in as near the same position as possible as he would have been but for the collision. If a yacht is damaged the owner is obliged to take all reasonable steps to minimise the loss, to save her from sinking, not to refuse reasonable offers of help from others, and not to unreasonably abandon her.

If a yacht is totally lost, the owner should recover the market value, although if she is fully insured he will be entitled to recover the full insured value (if more) from his insurers. When the yacht is not lost but damaged, the owner is entitled to recover the reasonable cost of repairs and expenses including salvage, towage charges, survey fees, and hauling out and relaunching charges. He is also entitled to the costs of repair even though, as in the case of renewal of sails, the end result may be an improvement in the condition and value of the vessel by a substitution of new for old materials.

When a vessel is put out of use for some time by damage, and a successful claim is made, other losses may also be added. If a yacht is being used for a commercial purpose, such as a training or charter yacht, the owner is entitled to compensation for his loss of earnings. In the case of the *Fortunity* [1960] 1 LL 252, a yacht built, owned and maintained solely for letting to the public on the Norfolk Broads, damages were assessed in this way. In the case of a privately used pleasure yacht, however, a court may simply award a sum equal to the loss of reasonable interest on the capital invested in the yacht during the time that the owner was deprived of her use. If of course the owner were to hire another comparable yacht while his own were under repair, his measure of damage for loss of use would be the sum paid for the hire, less any expenses which would have been common to both yachts.

Limitation of liability

One major difference between shipping law and other branches of the law is the right that is given to ship owners to limit their liability to persons who have suffered loss or damage, or even death or personal injury, as a result of the negligent navigation or management of the ship.

The principle of limitation goes back many centuries and is based on the impossibility of a ship owner being able to insure himself adequately against the potentially enormous claims that could arise from a maritime accident. The rules entitle the ship owner to calculate his potential liabilities by reference to the tonnage of his vessel. This, until recently, had an anomalous benefit for small yachts as was decided in the case of the *Annie Hay* in 1967. In that case the yacht *Annie Hay* collided with a motor cruiser in Falmouth Harbour causing damage worth £2700. The *Annie Hay* was found to be the boat at fault, but her owner claimed the right to limit his liability under the Merchant Shipping Acts to a sum of less than £200. The court held that he was entitled to, and thus resolved the uncertainty at that time as to whether the limitation of liability rule applied to pleasure yachts.

Under the rules in force in 1967 (later amended) the ship owner was entitled to limit his liability for property damage to a sum of £40 per ton, or where death or personal injury was involved, to £120 per ton subject to a minimum notional tonnage of 300 tons. Hence the owner of a yacht causing personal injury would never need, because of the limitation rules, to pay out more than 300 x £120 regardless of the damages that the court may have wished to award.

After 1 December 1986 new legislation, following a new International Convention, set the notional minimum tonnage at a much higher level, linked to International Units of Account (in 1993 equivalent to 80p per unit). For property damage an owner or skipper will not be able to limit below 83 333 Units of Account. For loss of life or personal injury the platform will be 166 667 Units of Account.

The most obvious consequence of these rules for pleasure sailors is that, despite the 1986 reforms, full damages for catastrophically serious injuries or incidents caused by the yacht will not be fully recoverable by the injured party.

Under the previous rules, the person entitled to claim liability was either the skipper or crew member of the vessel, or the owner. The 1976 Convention extended limitation to salvors of ships, and to any persons for whose action, neglect or default, the ship owner or salvor is responsible, as well as any insurer of liability for claims subject to limitation. The reason for the amendment regarding salvors was to enable them to limit their liability in circumstances such as arose in the case of the *Tojo Maru* [1971] 1 LL. In that case it was decided that the salvor could not limit his liability for negligence where a diver on salvage work caused an explosion by firing a bolt through plating into a tank that had not been freed of gas. His employers were unable to limit by reference to the tonnage of the salvage tug since the diver was not aboard at the time. The 1976 amendment allows a salvor to claim limitation when on board the vessel being salved.

Another important effect of the new rules is that the personal 'fault or privity' rule has been abolished in favour of a new standard for allowing limitation. Under the old rules an owner could not claim limitation if the Plaintiff could show that the damage was caused directly by the owner, rather than the skipper, engineer or other crew member acting on behalf of the owner. In other words, if the incident was caused by the owner's 'fault or privity', typically by his allowing the vessel to go to sea without adequate equipment, charts, or pilot books, or failing to pass important 'Notices to Mariners' on to the ship, then he would not be entitled to limit in the case of an incident.

The new rules replace the concept of 'fault or privity' with a provision that a ship owner will only be denied his right to limit 'if it is proved that the loss resulted from his personal act or omission, committed with the intent to cause such loss, or recklessly and with knowledge that such loss would probably result'.

The new wording effectively gives the ship owner very much more protection since in future a Plaintiff will have to show that there has been some element of maliciousness, and that it was the personal maliciousness of the person attempting to limit his liability. Therefore to overcome the limitation provision it must be proved by the Plaintiff, that the act or omission was a personal act or omission of the person liable, and furthermore that it was committed recklessly with knowledge that the loss would probably result.

At the time of writing there have been no cases in the English courts in which the Defendant has been denied the right to limit under the new rules; it is unlikely that the Plaintiff will be able to prove in any realistic circumstances that the owner or helmsman of the yacht should be able to limit his liability.

Despite the likelihood of liability for any marine accident being limited to a figure of around £200 000 (ie c £133 000 for death or personal injury and c £67 000 for property damage, arising from a single incident) most insurance companies now provide between £500 000 and £1m in third party indemnity cover.

The reason for this is that there are circumstances in which limitation may not be claimed. There are still a number of states where the Limitation Convention has not been brought into effect, and other states where it will not necessarily be applied to pleasure yachts. Since an injured party may well take legal action in one of these states, particularly if his vessel is of that nationality himself, or the incident took place in that state's territorial waters, full insurance is a sensible precaution.

Where an accident takes place aboard the insured pleasure yacht, and a guest or unpaid crew member is injured, limitation may not be claimed by the owner. Also, incidents occurring around the boat, perhaps in the boatyard or on a marina pontoon, will be covered by the yacht's insurance as 'liabilities arising by reason of the insured's interest in the vessel' but the insured will not be able to limit since accidents ashore are not covered by the Limitation Convention.

For this reason, and because, in this country at least, awards of damages together with legal costs may well approach £1m in the most serious cases, third party insurance to this level is now offered by most underwriters.

CHAPTER SEVEN

PUBLIC RIGHTS
OF NAVIGATION

Ownership of the seabed, and indeed the bed of all tidal waters, is vested in the Crown, or in some person or corporation to whom the Crown has granted title. There is however a presumed public right to navigate on all tidal waters, of such antiquity and importance that it takes precedence over the rights of the owner. This free public right of navigation extends as much to recreational craft as to merchant or naval craft, and may only be limited or interfered with in any way by a specific and unambiguous Act of Parliament, or a ministerial order made under the Transport and Works Act 1992.

Although the ebb and flow of the tide over a channel or creek is strong evidence of the existence of a public navigable waterway, whether there is a right of navigation depends very much on the exact situation of the waterway. The Earl of Ilchester took successful legal action in 1889 to prevent small boats disturbing his swans at high water springs, at Abbotsbury in Dorset, on the grounds that the creek was not accessible at normal tides and therefore the right of navigation did not extend to the upper part of the creek. Similarly, artificial cuttings, docks or marinas may also be closed to the public right although technically 'navigable' at all times.

The right to navigate is simply a right of way. It is a right to pass and repass and to anchor, similar to rights on a public road on land. On a highway the owner of a vehicle is allowed to drive, and to park for a reasonable time, but one must not permanently occupy a part of it. In the same way a yacht may anchor to wait for a favourable wind or tide, or to embark and disembark crew, but it probably may not occupy a part of the water as of right, or sink a permanent mooring without the consent of the owner of the bed.

In law the distinction between anchoring and mooring is not as clear as it may seem to the yacht owner. In the case of Attorney General v. Wright [1897] 2 QB 318 the question was considered at length and the view of the Court of Appeal was that a general right to lay fixed moorings was recognised by the law as a right which could be exercised against the owner of the bed. In this case a number of fishermen and yacht owners took action to prevent the lessee of a fishery from lifting fixed moorings that they had placed on the foreshore at Leigh-on-Sea. The lessee did not dispute that they had a right to anchor on the foreshore, but argued that they had no right to fix anything into the soil in a permanent way.

The court referred in its judgment to the two ways of mooring a vessel, either by anchoring or by picking up fixed moorings. 'Thus the yachts at Cowes Roads have moorings, which they take up whenever they return thereto, passing a chain or rope through the ring of the buoy, which indicates the mooring. There is therefore this mode of bringing a ship to rest and keeping her so for a time, within the ordinary course of navigation. This is not a right of any individual; it is a general right to use the waters for navigation in an ordinary way, and to anchor in either of the two well-known ways, either by means of an anchor, or to a mooring. Such a matter is not to be traced to a grant by the Sovereign, or the owner of the soil, but that it is a right by the law of England, a public right in everyone navigating in navigable waters. If so, the owner of the soil took his right to the soil subject to these general rights.'

In the more recent case of Fowley Marine (Emsworth) Limited v. Gafford [1968] 1 LL 343 the court reached a very different conclusion, reflecting perhaps the pressure that exists in modern times on mooring facilities. The court stated that there is no Common Law (ie general) right to lay or maintain permanent moorings, for it would 'be little less than fantastic that in the absence of statute or proved local custom the law should allow anyone navigating a ship or vessel, including every amateur yachtsman, to place bulky objects upon another person's land without permission and to retain them there, presumably forever, as being an ordinary incident of navigation'.

This decision has been subject to the criticism that the technical differences and similarities between anchoring and mooring were not fully examined by the court, and there is a body of legal opinion that believes that a properly presented case at some time in the future could re-establish the right to moor without the consent of the fundus owner. However in recent years most yacht owners, harbour authorities and yacht clubs have accepted that the owners of mooring areas should be paid a fee in return for the right to moor, and this may be a natural outcome of the changing yachting scene. Thus although the landlords' claim to be entitled to a rent is subject to some legal doubt, the practical difficulties of pursuing an expensive legal case, probably to a final appeal in the House of Lords, would be out of all proportion to the individual benefit that may accrue to boat owners; licence fees charged by the major public landlords at present tend to be modest. If they are increased in the future by an unreasonable amount, concerted action by mooring holders to re-determine their legal rights may become a viable option. Another aspect of the matter is that even if the mooring holders were successful in their claim, and the courts agreed that no rent was payable to the landlords, the loss of revenue to the public purse from the Crown Estate Commissioners mooring leases may well prompt an Act of Parliament to re-establish the right to charge to the ultimate detriment of the boat owning public.

This is not to say that cases may not arise from time to time when a mooring owner, or the holder of a block of moorings, may not have acquired rights under the Limitation Act. If he can show that he and his predecessor have enjoyed exclusive use of a mooring area for a period of time, and have done so without paying a rent or obtaining the landlord's consent, and in an open way without the use of force, he may well have acquired a statutory title to the mooring area. Since the Limitation Act 1980 requires a period of 12 years' uninterrupted use, the instances in which such a claim would be successful would obviously be very limited.

Consents required for providing moorings in tidal waters

As we have seen, it is generally accepted that the owner of the seabed can prevent a mooring being laid if he wishes to do so; to lay a mooring in defiance of the owner's wishes will normally be an act of trespass. There are however a number of other agencies whose consent may also be required including the Department of Transport, the local planning authority, and the harbour authority.

Department of Transport
Under Section 34 of the Coast Protection Act 1949 permission must be obtained from the Secretary of State for Transport before anything is placed below the high water mark which is, or may become, a danger to navigation. This includes mooring buoys.

The Merchant Shipping Act 1988 has amended this requirement by providing that where a harbour authority has the jurisdiction to license such works, the requirement to obtain consent from the Department of Transport will no longer apply in harbours where the Secretary of State has so directed (either at the request of the harbour authority concerned, or on his own initiative). The Coast Protection Act requires the Secretary of State, if he is of the opinion that any operation for which an application is made to him under Section 34 will cause, or is likely to result in, obstruction or danger to navigation, either to refuse consent or to give his consent subject to conditions imposed by him.

The scope of Section 34 was considered by the Court of Appeal in the case of Harwich Harbour Conservancy Board v. The Secretary of State for the Environment, East Suffolk County Council and Stour River Estate [1975] 1 AC 334. The question at issue was whether the Secretary of State, in considering whether to give his consent to the construction of a marina at Shotley, was entitled to take into account not only whether the proposed works would, in themselves, constitute an obstruction or danger to navigation (either directly or by causing siltation) but also whether the additional traffic which would be using the marina would obstruct or endanger navigation. It was held by the court that he could not refuse his consent simply on the grounds of the extra traffic that would be generated. However it was said by the court that possible obstruction by boats actively using the work, for example by boats tied up to a jetty, could be taken into account in considering such a case.

The limitation on the Secretary of State's jurisdiction has been removed by a new subsection inserted into the Coast Protection Act by the 1988 Merchant Shipping Act. This allows the Secretary of State to take into account any use intended to be made of the works in question when constructed, altered or improved.

Harbour authorities

At most harbours the authority's special legislation prohibits persons from constructing works below high water mark or dredging without first obtaining a licence from the harbour authority. In considering applications, the authority will be entitled to take into account not only navigational considerations, but also whether the proposed works are necessary or desirable for the trade in the port, and whether they will compete with facilities provided by the port authority itself. In all such cases the discretion of the authority must be exercised reasonably, failing which an application may be made to the High Court for judicial review.

Local planning authority

If the owner or user of land wishes to make a material change in the use of land, or seabed, this may constitute a development which requires planning permission. Before considering whether a particular activity involves a development within the planning law, it is first necessary to determine whether the area in question does actually lie within the jurisdiction of the local authority.

Local government areas are fixed, by the Local Government Act 1972, to a 'medium' low water mark. Effectively this is the point of low water on the day midway between neap and spring tides. Such areas also include 'accretions from the sea' and areas where the natural line of a watercourse has changed. The Town and Country Planning Act 1971 follows the same areas, and planning authorities generally have jurisdiction to that point. Below it, the sea is not subject to planning control.

So far as estuaries and arms of the sea are concerned the picture is rather less clear. Whether a river or arm of the sea is within the 'body of the county' depends upon the width of the river; in the case of the *Fagernes* [1927] P 311 the test was said to be whether a man on one shore could see what was done on the other. The onus of proof is on the person asserting that the land in question is within the county. The recipients of an enforcement notice from the local authority are therefore entitled to call on the Council to prove that the land covered by water is within their jurisdiction. If the proof is not forthcoming then the notice is invalid.

There are other aspects of the laying of moorings which might establish their permanence and therefore affect their status as 'developments'. For example, some types of moorings depend on concrete blocks or discs, with an anchor bar to which the mooring chain is fixed, dug into the mud. Where a mooring weight simply rests on the bottom it is less likely that this would amount to development, since it is the use of the land that is relevant, and a mooring weight does not interfere with the land itself. Thus it would not be a development to leave the boat at its own anchor, or mud weight, and it becomes a matter of degree at what stage the size of the weight makes it a development. Although the matter has not been tested in court in recent years, it may be that the test applied in the 1984 Rates Act for the rating of moorings may be applied, namely that moorings which are designed to be raised from time to time for the purposes of inspection and maintenance are deemed to be insufficiently permanent to be charged rates, and by the same token should be regarded as insufficiently permanent to constitute a 'development'.

Restrictions on navigation rights

Marine nature reserves

The growth in recent years of public awareness of the damage done to the environment by unchecked activity or other irresponsible use of the sea has led to increasing pressures for controls over sea areas. Such bodies as English Nature, the Royal Society for the

Protection of Birds and the Marine Conservation Society have quite properly raised public awareness of these issues, not least among recreational boat owners who perhaps have the most powerful of all vested interests in keeping the sea wholesome. In recent years particular pressure has been put on the Government by environmental pressure groups for the introduction of a scheme of integrated coastal zone management, whereby the jurisdiction of the many different local, county and central government agencies that overlap in the coastal zone would be subject to the overall policy control of a single co-ordinating agency. The response of central government to these pressures has been that the present system of controls, which provides checks and balances in conserving sensitive parts of the coastline, while at the same time permitting necessary development subject to strict controls, is a workable system. However, continuing initiatives by the major environmental bodies, many of whom see the public right of navigation as a threat to the interests they wish to protect, will inevitably increase pressures to reduce public rights and prevent access to certain parts of the coast. This already happens in certain areas between the Frisian Islands and the mainland coast of Holland and Germany, and is a cause enthusiastically supported by the European Commission.

Many inter-tidal mooring areas are now designated as environmentally protected areas. With the increase in recreational boating, controls on antifouling paints and the release of raw sewage, and dumping of refuse in general, are very necessary.

English Nature is responsible for the designation of areas of significance under the following categories:

- Sites of Special Scientific Interest
- Wetlands of International Importance under the Ramsar Convention
- Special Protection Areas

In addition, there are local nature reserves, some with their own byelaws that prohibit anchoring, such as within Pagham Harbour, and Marine Nature Reserves established under the Wildlife and Countryside Act 1981. Under that Act byelaws may be made by English Nature excluding pleasure craft from certain parts of Marine Nature Reserves at certain times of the year. Such byelaws have been introduced to restrict vessels from mooring and anchoring within certain areas around Lundy and Skomer Islands, and certain proposals are under consideration for parts of the Menai Straits.

Ministry of Defence

Apart from control of wide areas of sea and estuarial waters comprising the Naval Ports, the Ministry of Defence also controls, through the Property Services Agency, extensive areas for gunnery or bombing practice, or as proving ranges. During firing times these areas, which are marked out on the relevant Admiralty charts, are patrolled by MoD police who are entitled to request passing traffic to keep clear of certain limits. While it is in everyone's interest to comply with such requests so far as possible, there is however no range in the United Kingdom where the authorities have the right to exclude vessels passing from one side to another, and taking no longer than is reasonably necessary to do so. All range byelaws are carefully worded so as to preserve the bona fide right to transit the range at any time, even though firing might be scheduled and the military subjected to delay or inconvenience. This right applies as much to recreational craft as to others, provided there is no unreasonable delay in crossing. The question has arisen as to whether a yacht racing to a turning mark in the middle of a gunnery range area is entitled to sail in, round the mark, and sail out the way it had come in. Since the byelaws specifically exempt vessels 'crossing' the sea area, it seems clear that a yacht on a course involving a U-turn in the middle of the sea area would not be able to claim the exemption.

Oyster fisheries

The Ministry of Agriculture, Fisheries and Food has powers under the Sea Fisheries Acts to make orders establishing oyster and mussel fisheries. Such orders give exclusive rights to the individuals or companies in whose favour they are made. It is a trespass to interfere with an oyster or mussel bed, including the placing of any apparatus prejudicial to the bed (such as a mooring) except for the purpose of navigation or anchorage. It should be noted that the right to anchor does not include the right to lay a mooring; nor does it include the right to drag one's anchor. In *The Swift* [1901] P 168, the oyster bed owners successfully took proceedings against the owners of a vessel which had dragged its anchor over the beds. The position is that the right of navigation is paramount but must be exercised reasonably and a grounding without the legal right to do so is a trespass to the owner of the seabed.

Inland waters
So far as inland waters are concerned, there are public rights of navigation on certain rivers, canals and lakes, but there is no general right of navigation on all water, and each case must be considered individually.

Rivers
In the case of natural rivers, whether it is subject to public rights depends in the first place on whether it is physically possible for craft to use it, and secondly whether there is a legal right to do so.

Our rivers have always been important for a variety of reasons, including water supply, agriculture, fisheries, public health, and navigation. As well as providing lines of communication they provided power for corn, wool and iron mills before the days of steam. In mediaeval times when roads were poor, inland navigation rights were particularly important and bitter disputes occurred between those who wanted free navigation for their vessels and the owners of mills and fisheries who depended on the building of dams, weirs and the like.

Legal rights to navigation can be created (in the same way as for a highway on dry land) by ancient usage, by express or implied dedication by the owner, or by a statute creating a new right or confirming an existing common law right.

The bed of a non-tidal river will normally belong to the owners of the adjacent land (the riparian owners) and there is in this country no general legal right to pass over (whether on foot or by boat) another person's land. One way in which the public right can be acquired is by immemorial user. In theory this means that the river has been used by the public since 1189 (the year of the death of King Henry II and the historical limit of English legal memory). In practice it is sufficient to prove that a river has been used by the public without the express permission of the riparian owners for as long as anyone can remember; in such a case the right will be deemed to have existed since 1189.

There is no doubt that on many rivers the public does enjoy the right to navigate for considerable distances upstream as a result of such historical usage. Certainly this applies to such major rivers as the Severn, Thames, Ouse, Trent, Medway, Nene and Witham, and to a number of lesser rivers, and is also claimed to exist on a great deal more. Public rights on the major rivers are generally well documented, and the majority of boat owners are content to limit their cruising to those canals and rivers where there is no dispute as to rights. However the growth in touring by canoes, and in the number of canal and river restoration projects, has given rise to an increasing number of conflicts.

In the Yorkshire Derwent case [1992] 1 AER 230 the House of Lords finally closed the door on a possible major extension of navigation rights throughout the country. Overturning a Court of Appeal decision, the court held that the 1932 Rights of Way Act, which confers public rights of way after as little as 20 years of public use, does not apply to rivers. Although common law rights of navigation arose out of the need in past centuries to use the rivers as a means of transport for commercial purposes, recent cases show that where the right of navigation exists it includes the right to navigate for the purposes of recreation. In the Cairngorm case [1977] it was held that canoeists were entitled to enjoy the public right of navigation on a river even though it may originally

Public rights of navigation on inland waterways are enshrined in ancient statutes.

have been established for a commercial purpose.

Public rights may also be created by an Act of Parliament. In the 17th and 18th centuries developers were frequently authorised by private statute to improve the navigation on rivers, or to make passable those that were previously not navigable, for example the Wey, the Rother, the Avon and the Upper Avon. In the case of statutes for the improvement of rivers, the developers would be given the necessary legal powers to carry out the improvements, although they were not then specifically required to do so. If they did in fact carry out improvements under their Act, the river would thereby become dedicated to the public (the 1699 River Trent Navigation Act refers to 'All the King's liege people whatsoever') and the promoters were bound to apply the profits from the navigation tolls for the future benefit of the public using the navigation. They were, in effect, trustees for the public interest, and most of today's navigation authorities including British Waterways, the National Rivers Authority, the National Trust, and the other controlling bodies, are the inheritors of that role.

A statute conferring a public right of navigation may of course be repealed by a subsequent Act of Parliament. Ministers of the Crown also have the right to make orders repealing or amending enactments affecting navigation, under the Land Drainage Acts, the Water Acts, and the Transport and Works Acts. However the repeal of a statute conferring a statutory right of navigation would not of itself abolish any pre-existing common law rights of navigation.

Where there is no right to navigate, any attempt to do so will constitute a trespass. In the case of Rawson v. Peters [1972] an incursion by a canoeist into a valuable angling beat, even though it was not being fished on the day in question, was held to be an actionable trespass giving rise to damages and an injunction to prevent further trespass. On the question of interference with fishing rights, Lord Denning said 'It did not matter that there was no-one fishing at the time. If the canoeing interfered with the right to fish minutes or hours afterwards there would be interference; the passage of canoes up and down the river must disturb the fish and interfere with fishing, therefore the rights of the angling club had been interfered with.'

The case reflects a principle that affects even those rivers on which a public right of navigation exists, namely that it must be exercised reasonably, and only by craft of a size that can sensibly use the river. The imposition by the National Trust of a 25 hp limit on motor boats using the River Wey is an example of how one navigation authority interprets this principle, and surprisingly this arbitrary limit has not yet been subject to legal challenge.

A right of navigation on water does not, of itself, give a right to go ashore, to moor, or to tow along the banks. One may land and embark only at the places provided, and where it is a non-tidal waterway there is no public right to fish. It is doubtful whether a right to anchor is an incident of the right of navigation in a non-tidal waterway, unless in the case of necessity or where custom has established it.

Canals

Although canal construction did not begin in earnest in this country until the 17th century, the Romans had developed several British navigations, including the still navigable Fossdyke in Lincolnshire. A number of rivers were later canalised and made navigable by Act of Parliament, but our statutory navigations are for the most part canals proper, being artificial waterways constructed by Parliamentary authority.

A typical canal Act gives power to the developer to acquire the land by compulsory purchase, to build the canal, and then to admit the public at large on payment of the statutory tolls. It is this latter section that contains the dedication to the public of a right of way for boats over the canal. There will also be a duty to keep it in reasonable repair (if it is not expressed it will be implied). The Act will also impose other requirements such as a duty to fence the canal banks, accept drainage from neighbouring properties, construct and maintain accommodation works, and establish free wharfs for the benefit of towns and villages along the canal.

These duties were generally ignored, and fell into disuse, after the coming of the railways in the 19th century. When a railway company promoted an Act of Parliament it usually met opposition from the nearby canal companies which the railways would have to buy out. Thus the railways acquired extensive canal interests which they thereafter largely neglected, although they could be forced by legal injunction to keep the navigation in repair and operational.

On the nationalisation of the railways in 1947 over 2000 miles of waterways were vested in the British Transport Commission, which later passed into the control of the British Waterways Board by the Transport Act 1964. The present legislation imposes a number of duties on the Board, including the maintenance of those canals designated as Commercial Waterways and Cruising Waterways; a further category of Remainder Waterways gives the Board permissive powers to restore derelict or semi-derelict canals, and this power is often exercised in conjunction with the many enthusiastic voluntary groups that have been working in recent years to restore and re-establish old navigations.

The 1991 British Waterways Bill (which at the time of writing had yet to be enacted) is intended to give the Board a wide variety of new powers deemed to be necessary for the efficient management of the navigation in modern terms. The legislation includes powers to control houseboats, to prohibit long-term moorings except in designated places, to license mooring structures, and to require all craft to have third party insurance and to comply with strict construction and equipment regulations with periodic surveys.

The Norfolk and Suffolk Broads

This enclosed system of rivers and artificial lakes which covers some 2600 acres with over 100 miles of waterways, contains a mix of waters with a public right of navigation, and private water.

A claim to navigation rights on the Broads will depend, in most cases, on proof of the tidal nature of the disputed water. The issue was raised in the case of Blower v. Ellis [1886] 50 JP 326. This concerned Wroxham Broad, 38 miles from the sea. The Appellant had been convicted of fishing in private water but argued on appeal that the Broads was part of the River Bure, which at one time was an arm of the sea where the tide ebbed and flowed. The court held that the Broad was not part of the River Bure, was not tidal, and was not a public navigation.

Public rights on lakes

Since a natural lake is really no more than a slow-moving wide river, public rights of navigation can be built up over a period of time in much the same way as a normal river. Llangorse Lake in the Brecon Beacons is an example of a lake which has long enjoyed an alleged public right of navigation for commercial purposes, but where the owner of the lake bed contends that the right, if it existed at all, was only for the purpose of going from a point of departure to a point of destination, and did not include the right for small craft being used for recreational purposes to use the water in a random way without a specific destination being intended.

In the Lake District an undisputed public right of navigation exists over the full length of four of the lakes (Windermere, Coniston, Ullswater and Derwent Water) which all come under the control of the National Parks Authority. The fact that the right of navigation is not absolute is well illustrated by the policy of the Lake District Special Planning Board in pressing for a 10 mph speed limit for Lake Windermere. Their original proposals, circulated in the late 1980s to promote an Act of Parliament to revoke the common law right of navigation and to replace it with limited rights to navigate certain craft at certain times, was withdrawn after adverse public reaction. A later proposal simply to impose a speed limit by byelaw would not prejudice public rights of navigation and indeed is well precedented in most harbours and on most rivers and canals around the country. Although there are historic reasons for allowing organised motor boat racing and other similar activities over parts of the lake, the right to navigate does not automatically imply the right to navigate at high speed, or even the right to waterski.

CHAPTER EIGHT

FLAG LAW

In an era when the barriers between states are coming down between members of the European Community, the concept of a national flag required by law to be flown on every sea-going vessel can seem somewhat dated.

The flying of flags is governed in part by International Convention and Government legislation, and in part by custom and tradition. So far as British ships are concerned (and the legal definition of 'ship' is any vessel used in navigation, not propelled by oars), the 1894 Merchant Shipping Act, Section 73, lays down that the Red Ensign shall be the proper national colours. Section 74 of the Act also requires any vessel of over 50 registered tons to wear her national colours on entering or leaving port.

Although registration on the British Register is no longer compulsory for yachts, following the 1988 Merchant Shipping Act which replaced the obligation with 'entitlement', international law still requires all foreign-going craft to be registered. Article 5 of the 1958 Geneva Convention on the High Seas provides that:

'Each state shall fix the conditions for the grant of nationality to ships, for the registration of ships in its territory, and for the right to fly its flag. Ships have the nationality of the state whose flag they are entitled to fly. There must exist a genuine link between the state and the ship; in particular the state must effectively exercise its jurisdiction and control in administrative, technical and social matters over ships flying its flag. Each state shall issue ships to which it has granted the right to fly its flag documents to that effect.'

The Convention has been adopted by all the leading maritime nations of the world, most of which require foreign ships visiting their waters to fly their flags for the purpose of identification. The Convention also requires them to carry valid registration documents abroad to prove the right to fly the flag. Thus, although registration is no longer compulsory in this country for yachts staying in UK waters, it is a legal requirement for visiting overseas states.

Privileged ensigns

In addition to the Red Ensign, yachts belonging to members of certain yacht clubs may also wear the White Ensign, the plain or defaced Blue Ensign, or the defaced Red Ensign. There are some 70 privileged clubs in the United Kingdom, and a number overseas in the former colonies and the Republic of Ireland. Prior to 1983 the privilege was limited to craft entered on the Part I Register of Shipping who were entitled to apply to the Admiralty for a personal warrant to fly a special ensign. Defence budget cuts in that year would have resulted in the scrapping of the system had the Ministry of Defence proposals been followed, but a new scheme was agreed with the Royal Yachting Association. Under this scheme each privileged club in the UK obtained a club warrant from the Ministry, and became entitled to issue individual permits to members whose boats were registered either on the Part I Register or on the Small Ships Register.

There were fears expressed at the time that the replacement of the Admiralty Warrant with a simple permit would reduce demand for the privilege, but the 70 clubs have retained a total permit issue of over 10 000, so demand was clearly unaffected by the new arrangements.

In 1983 the Admiralty Board decided that the list of privileged clubs would only be extended in exceptional circumstances, and since then only the Royal Findhorn Yacht Club has been added to the list. This does not however prevent individual clubs from applying direct to the Sovereign for an award of the privilege which remains in the royal prerogative. The award in 1987 of the unique sky blue ensign, defaced with the RAF roundel, to the Royal Air Force Sailing Association is an example of the royal prerogative circumventing standard Admiralty Board procedures.

An unsuccessful attempt to turn the system to commercial advantage led to the dispute over the Royal Corinthian Yacht Club ensign at Cowes in 1989. The main agents in the UK for Beneteau Yachts negotiated the purchase of this prestigious yacht club's building, in the mistaken belief that in buying the premises it would thereby be buying the club, and with it the right to award privileged ensign permits to its customers who would be given membership of the club.

In the legal proceedings which followed, the company eventually accepted that all it had purchased was the clubhouse itself; the club being an unincorporated members' association is not a legal entity and is thus not capable of being bought or sold, and consequently there was no right either to continue to call the premises 'Royal Corinthian Yacht Club', nor to offer customers membership of the club or the right to wear the Blue Ensign.

Even if the club and ensign had changed hands with the transfer of the clubhouse, the use of the ensign for commercial purposes would have been contrary to the regulations governing use of the flag. The flag may not even be used for advertising purposes, and the owner of a racing yacht at a regatta was threatened with expulsion from his club for wearing a Blue Ensign at the stern of his yacht and a sponsor's logo printed across his spinnaker, while returning to his mooring after a race.

The White Ensign

The use of the senior flag is limited to the Royal Navy and the 600 members of the Royal Yacht Squadron whose yachts (both sail and power) are regarded in theory as naval reserve craft, subject to call-up in times of national emergency. There was once the belief that such craft were entitled to the privileges of ships of the Royal Navy even when not in service. In 1922 a yacht flying the White Ensign, entering Dover Harbour at night, struck an unmarked wreck and the owner sued the harbour master alleging breach of his statutory duty to keep the entrance safe. The defence alleged that the yacht was in breach of a statutory order prohibiting any vessels 'other than His Majesty's ships' from using the eastern entrance of the harbour during darkness without the authority of the harbour master. This yacht had no such authority, but it was argued that as the yacht was flying the White Ensign it should be treated as one of His Majesty's ships. This argument found no favour with the court, the judge declaring 'The sooner those who own yachts, whether members of the Royal Yacht Squadron or not, disabuse themselves of the idea that these craft stand in the position of one of His Majesty's ships the better it will be for them and the better for safe navigation generally'.

The Blue Ensign

In plain (undefaced) form this is the ensign of the Royal Naval Reserve and Auxiliary ships, and the next most senior clubs after the Royal Yacht Squadron. At the top of the list comes the Royal Thames Yacht Club, with the Royal Motor Yacht Club and the

Sussex Motor Yacht Club close behind in seniority. Only some 20 clubs in the country enjoy this privilege.

Thirty-nine clubs are permitted to wear Blue Ensigns 'defaced' with a club badge. Amongst these are the Thames Motor Yacht Club at Hampton Court (awarded the privilege in honour of the heroism of their members' 'little ships' at Dunkirk), the Royal Corinthian Yacht Club, and the Bar Yacht Club.

The defaced Red Ensign

A group of 10 clubs at the bottom of the privilege list are entitled to Red Ensigns defaced with the club badge. These include the House of Commons Yacht Club and the Lloyd's Yacht Club.

Arguments about the seniority of clubs can be endless, but by common consent the most senior club in age in the British Isles is in fact the Royal Cork Yacht Club, established in 1726. The club flag now wears the tricolour of the Republic of Ireland in place of the Union Flag, but the warrant to fly the flag is as valued as much now as it was in the days of British rule.

Prevention of abuse

A common cause of concern among British yacht owners cruising overseas is the apparent widespread abuse of the Red or Blue Ensign on vessels that are obviously foreign-owned. In most cases it is likely that the use of the flag is in fact quite legitimate. Under the Merchant Shipping Act, 1993 any ship may be registered on the Part I Register provided the owner has an established link with the United Kingdom (or the Channel Islands or the Isle of Man). Thus all that is required for any overseas national is to establish a brass-plate company in the British Isles and transfer ownership of the ship to that company. The wearing of the Red Ensign thus becomes entirely lawful. At a time when the majority of British-owned commercial shipping is being 'flagged out' to other countries whose rules on construction, manning and equipment are less stringent, and very much cheaper to comply with, it may seem strange that foreign yacht owners wish to 'flag in' to the United Kingdom. The answer is of course to be found in the very low level of regulations applying to pleasure craft in the UK used for private purposes. Whereas other states have regulations covering design, construction and equipment, annual taxation and licensing of drivers, very few rules apply in the UK or to British registered yachts; the initial registration fee and annual administrative charge for the holding company are relatively cheap by comparison.

Where abuses do occur, either by the improper wearing of a

A Port Health Authority vessel carrying a defaced Blue Ensign with the coat of arms of the Corporation of London on the fly. In addition, she carries a St George flag with a red dagger, symbol of the City of London, in the upper left hand canton of the hoist.

defaced ensign by a British national, or the improper wearing of a Red Ensign by a foreign national, Section 73 of the Merchant Shipping Act 1894 provides the remedy. Any commissioned officer on full pay in the military or naval service of Her Majesty, or any officer of Customs in Her Majesty's dominions, or any British Consular Officer, may board the ship on which any colours or pendant are being unlawfully worn, and seize and take away the colours which shall be forfeited to Her Majesty.

The European Community

Although the Geneva Convention on the High Seas states that a vessel automatically takes the nationality of its owner and must wear the colours of the owner's state of nationality, the decision of the European Court in the *Factortame* case (1991 – C – 246/89) is in direct conflict with this rule. Since the European Court's decision, many EC nationals resident in Great Britain have registered their yachts on the British registers. The 1993 Merchant Shipping Act, introduced as a result of the *Factortame* case, provides that any EC national resident in the UK may register his vessel on the Small Ships Register, and any EC national established (ie with a home or business) in the UK may register his vessel on the Part I Register. No doubt the Geneva Convention will be amended in due course to recognise this lowering of the barriers around Europe.

Another factor eroding the status of national ensigns within Europe is the increasingly common practice of flying the 'Euro-Ensign'. This is no more than the European Community's blue flag with gold stars. Though popular as a yacht ensign, this flag has no official status and in law it is no substitute for a national ensign.

CHAPTER 9

INSURANCE

Although there is as yet no general legislation requiring pleasure craft to carry insurance, a number of harbour authorities, marina companies, and inland navigation authorities insist on third party insurance as do most yacht clubs for members racing or using club moorings and finance houses lending money on the security of a yacht. The 1991 British Waterways Bill was the first Bill in Parliament to introduce a third party insurance requirement for pleasure craft using the rivers and canals under BW control, and with the successful introduction of that regime, it would only be a matter of time before compulsory insurance applies nationwide.

Prior to 1986, the Merchant Shipping Act allowed the owner of a yacht which caused a collision to limit his liability for any resulting damage to property to £40 per registered ton. Although the limit for causing death or personal injury was very much higher, many owners of older yachts were content to remain uninsured in the knowledge that even if they were to sink another vessel, provided no death or personal injury ensued, they would only have to pay a few hundred pounds' compensation.

Since 1986, when very much higher limits came into effect, the risks of being uninsured have increased greatly, and in practice there are very few privately owned pleasure yachts in the country that do not carry full insurance, let alone insurance against third party risks.

Insurable interest

A valid contract of insurance cannot be made unless the insured has an actual interest in the yacht. An insurance policy without an actual interest would be a simple wager, or bet, and therefore unenforceable at law. An interest can be vested in the owner, charterer, mortgagee or even the holder of a lien over the yacht.

The Marine Insurance Act 1906 provides the following definition of insurable interest.

1   Subject to the provisions of this Act, every person has an insurable interest who is interested in a marine adventure.

2   In particular, a person is interested in a marine adventure where he stands in any legal or equitable relation to the adventure or to any insurable property at risk therein, in consequence of which he may benefit by the safety or due arrival of insurable property, or may be prejudiced by its loss, or by damage thereto, or by the detention thereof, or may incur liability in respect thereof.

A contingent interest may be insurable as provided by Section 7 of the Act. When a yacht is being sold and delivered to the buyer it is often agreed in the contract that she should remain at the seller's risk until arrival at the port chosen by the buyer. For the seller to get his money in full, the yacht has to arrive in the same condition as she set out and it is his responsibility to see that she is insured. When the risk of the voyage is on the seller, the buyer will not have an insurable interest in the yacht during the voyage.

This question arose in Piper v. Royal Exchange Assurance [1932] 44 LL 103. In that case the yacht *Atalanta II* was bought in Norway for delivery to Essex. During the voyage she suffered damage resulting in a claim against the underwriters by the purchaser. The underwriters paid out, but were later found by the Court of Appeal to be entitled to repayment since the contract of sale had provided that the yacht would be at the seller's risk, not the buyer's, during the voyage.

Valuation

Unlike motor insurance, where the value of the car in the event of a write-off is taken to be its current market value, marine insurance is based on the principle of agreed value. If a yacht is insured for, say, £10 000, and in the case of a total loss the underwriters are able to show that it would have fetched no more than £8000 on the open market, they are still liable to pay the full figure. However the valuation put on the vessel by the assured is important not only because it has a direct bearing on the premium to be charged, but because a substantial over-valuation could be construed as an intentional attempt to deceive and could, in a serious case, make the policy void.

In the case of Slattery v. Mance [1962] 1 QB 676, the yacht *Trewarval Light*, insured for £4500 under a Lloyd's policy, suffered a total loss by fire when moored in the River Seine, near Lavencourt. The underwriters rejected the claim on the grounds that the value of the yacht had been overstated in the proposal form. They relied particularly on the fact that the owner had been prepared to accept an offer of £2850 a few days before he completed the proposal form showing a value of £4500. The judge advised the jury that the true commercial value on the market must be regarded as elastic, but it did seem unbelievable to say it could have increased by this sum in a few days. The jury held that the representation of value was an untrue and material misrepresentation and the underwriters therefore avoided liability.

On most modern proposal forms for marine insurance, separate questions are asked as to the price paid, and value. There is no reason why these should not be different, but the answer to the former question should be strictly factual, while the answer to the latter may reflect the owner's subjective opinion as to the value. In any event, if there is a substantial difference between the two figures, the owner should be prepared to give a full explanation.

The proposal form

The first step in insuring a yacht will usually be to contact one or more insurance brokers or companies who will each send a proposal form setting out the terms offered and the various restrictions and modifications under which cover will be provided. The form will call for full particulars of the vessel, her engines, designed speed, what use she will be put to, waters to be sailed and when and where she will be laid up. Particulars will also be asked about her fire extinguishers, tender and liferaft, outboard motors and other loose equipment, the experience and qualifications of the owner and other people likely to sail her, any adverse insurance history, and what size of excess is to be carried. In particular, insurers will wish to know if the yacht is to be raced, to be sailed single-handed, let out on charter or used for any commercial purpose.

When completing the proposal form the owner should bear in mind that any misrepresentation, or inadequate or false information, may entitle the underwriters to deny all liability under the policy in the event of a claim being made. Section 33 of the Marine

Insurance Act provides that any statement by which the assured promises to do, or not to do, something, or asserts a particular state of facts, must be exactly complied with, whether it is material to the risk or not. If it is not complied with, the insurer is discharged from liability. In theory this means that every time an underwriter receives a claim, he is entitled to go through the proposal form with a fine-tooth comb to check that every word in it is true, and every statement of intent has been followed through. If not, even if the statement, act or omission has nothing to do with the claim, he is entitled to reject the claim. In practice, underwriters in general take a more pragmatic attitude, and will pay out if they are satisfied that the claim is bona fide, and arises from one of the insured perils.

Since the proposal form does not constitute a contractual offer, the proposer is in no way bound by filling in and signing a proposal form. Indeed a new owner would be wise to shop around the insurance market to look for the best quotation. However value for money cannot be judged by the size of the premium alone; the record of the insurance companies when it comes to full, prompt and 'quibble-free' payouts varies enormously, and personal recommendations from owners of similar yachts who have had to make a claim on their policies can be valuable.

The standard policy

Even though Lloyd's underwriters no longer dominate the market as before, most yacht insurance policies available in the United Kingdom are based on the Lloyd's Institute Yacht Clauses. The standard form policy is subjected to minor revisions from time to time, but nonetheless still remains barely comprehensible to the layman. Since the policy can only be fully understood when read in conjunction with the 1906 Marine Insurance Act, and the substantial body of decided cases contained in the Lloyd's Law Reports, the layman is further confounded.

However it must be remembered that yacht insurance policies are based very much on the tried and tested ship insurance policies which go back over two centuries and although the terms may be quite incomprehensible to the uninitiated, each paragraph, sentence and phrase has been analysed and interpreted in court, and thus has a definite and agreed meaning. This level of complexity is required since, by comparison with say a motor car or private house, the risks to which a yacht is subject are infinitely more variable, and the underwriters will understandably wish to limit their liability to occurrences which are caused by some external accidental cause, while the yacht is being used within the area, by known

This sailor is limping back home to check his insurance policy. Are racing risks covered?

persons, and for the purpose declared on the proposal form.

The policy is a contractual document comprising a number of conditions binding upon the assured, upon compliance with which the insurer will indemnify the assured in the event of a loss occurring within the cover provided by the policy.

Since the Marine Insurance Act also implies some conditions into insurance contracts, the contract consists of a number of implied terms (ie those contained in the Marine Insurance Act) and a number of express terms (ie those contained in the written insurance policy).

Implied terms

Although most of the implied terms are designed to protect the interests of the insurer, there are two provisions which operate in favour of the assured.

Section 55 of the Act provides that the insurer is liable for any loss proximately caused by a peril insured against, and that he is liable even if the negligence of the owner was a contributory factor. Thus in the case of a yachtsman who carelessly left his yacht in a potentially exposed anchorage and went ashore without listening to a weather forecast, the insurance company was required to pay since the proximate cause of the loss was not the negligence of the owner, but the action of the elements in driving the yacht ashore.

Section 39 of the Act also provides that, unless the insurance policy specifically refers to seaworthiness, there is no implied warranty by the owner that the vessel is in a seaworthy state throughout the period of the insurance, although if he knowingly takes the yacht to sea in an unseaworthy state, the insurer will not be liable for any loss attributed to that fact.

So far as the insurer is concerned, the fundamental legal principle governing claims is that it is for the claimant to prove that the loss or damage was caused by an insured peril.

In the case of the *Tropaioforos* [1960] 2 LL 469, a vessel sank in a calm sea. The ship owners alleged that she had struck a submerged object, but the insurers contended that the loss was not due to perils of the sea, and that she had been deliberately scuttled. The judge stated that the claimant has the burden of proof that there was an accidental loss, on the balance of probabilities. One reason for this is that the ship owner has all, or almost all, the relevant information, and the insurers are likely to have no information at all, initially.

The second fundamental principle implied by the Act (Rule 7 of the Rules for Construction of the Policy) is that the damage must be attributed to some external, accidental cause, and not simply be the result of ordinary wear and tear, lack of maintenance or the ordinary action of the winds and waves. In the case of Wadsworth Lighterage v. Sea Insurance Co Ltd (1929) 34 LL Rep 285 a steam barge over 50 years old sank in dock in Liverpool. No one was around at the time and there was no apparent cause for the sinking. The insurers refused to pay, and the Court of Appeal found in their favour. Section 55 of the Marine Insurance Act provides that 'Unless the policy otherwise provides, the insurer is not liable for ordinary wear and tear', and the court found nothing in the contract of insurance to the contrary. The fact that the vessel sank, was not the point; only where a sinking occurred as a result of an insured peril, would the claim be enforceable.

By the same principle, if a lightly built or lightly rigged yacht is taken to sea in obviously unsuitable conditions, the loss for instance of the mast may well not be covered since such a loss could be regarded as inevitable. Indeed in the case of some older yachts, insurers will only provide cover for rig damage in wind strengths up to a certain level.

The same principle has been held to apply in the case of yachts with old (and externally sound) wooden masts suffering glued joint failure in relatively mild conditions. For a claim to be paid, the insured must be able to point to an external accidental cause resulting in damage, be it a freak wave, an unusually and unexpectedly strong squall, flotsam in the water, or some breakage on the yacht causing subsequent further damage. If all the assured is able to do is to say the yacht sank, or the rig collapsed, with no evidence that it was the result of a fortuity, then the underwriter will normally not be obliged to pay.

The underwriter is however not entitled to rely on broken equipment or rigging, or even inadequate construction, as a reason for rejecting a claim in every case. In the case of *Miss Jay Jay* [1987] 1 LL 32 a lightly built motor cruiser on passage from Deauville to Hamble encountered confused and difficult seas, in weather conditions that were described as brisk but not extreme. The bow section of the yacht was extensively damaged by continuous pounding over a period of some hours, although no damage was found until the yacht arrived at Hamble. The underwriters rejected the claim, saying that the damage was caused by poor construction. The judge rejected this argument saying that, while poor construction was not in doubt, the actual damage was caused by adverse weather conditions, and therefore the claim was valid.

Express terms

In general terms the standard policy contains three principal areas of cover as follows:

1   Loss of, or damage to, a craft caused by some external accidental means. This includes sinking, stranding, fire, collision, theft of the vessel, and theft of her contents or fittings (provided force was used in entering the vessel by the thief). The cover is provided whether the vessel is in commission or laid up; in the latter case accidents during towing, docking and shoring up will also be covered.

2   Damage caused to third parties, whether property damage to other craft or jetties, or personal injury (or death) to other individuals. Also covered is legal liability for injury or loss occurring to guests or unpaid crew aboard the yacht. This is of particular importance since the Merchant Shipping Act Limitation of Liability provisions do not extend to injury sustained on the owner's own vessel, and thus any sum awarded in damages by the courts will have to be paid in full. This section also covers any legal costs involved in defending actions against the owner arising out of any cause connected with his ownership of the yacht. The standard policy extends this section to the costs involved in the raising and disposal of the wreck of the vessel, which would be relevant if a harbour authority was put to that expense if a yacht sunk within their area of jurisdiction.

3 Salvage charges claimed by salvors for preventing a loss by
   perils insured against.

As we have seen, the standard policy contains a number of limitations or conditions, referred to as warranties, most of which are
designed to protect the insurer's interests. An important warranty in the Institute Yacht Clauses is that the designed speed of
the vessel is not over 17 knots. If it were, the policy would have
to be subjected to the Speedboat Clauses, which provide a list of
additional requirements again designed to protect the insurer's
position.

There will also be a warranty that the vessel will only be used
for private pleasure purposes and not let out on hire or charter
unless specifically agreed. A similar warranty applies to use for
racing, since the risk of damage between racing yachts is very
much higher than for cruising.

Most insurance policies carry a prohibition on the vessel being
used as a houseboat without the express consent of the underwriters. In the case of *Moonacre* [1992] 2 LL 501 the owner of a 78 foot
motor yacht insured his craft with a British underwriter and took
his yacht to Puerto Banus in Spain for a couple of seasons. The proposal form stated dates for which the yacht would be in commission and dates on which she would be laid up. Although the yacht
was laid up, and under Customs seal, at the appropriate time the
owner had a paid hand living aboard, and he himself was aboard
much of the time, working on the refurbishment of the yacht.
When a fire damaged the yacht the underwriters refused to pay
out on the grounds that she was being used as a houseboat. The
court held that living aboard a yacht that was not in commission at
the time did constitute use as a houseboat and accordingly the
underwriters were entitled to avoid the claim. In that case, however, the owner was able to recover equal damages from his broker
who had negligently failed to advise him that living on the yacht
while she was laid up would invalidate the policy.

A further interesting aspect of this case was the attempt by the
underwriters to avoid the claim on the additional grounds that the
yacht was registered in the name of a limited company (as a means
of minimising the owner's tax liabilities). Their claim that the
owner did not have an insurable interest was rejected by the court
on the grounds that he was the sole shareholder in the company
and was therefore the beneficial owner of the yacht. However,
owners registering their yachts in the name of a limited company,
a common enough occurrence, would be well advised to advise
their insurers of the exact position.

The limits of the cruising range, and the dates stated for being in
commission and laid up are also regarded by the insurers as being

of fundamental importance, breach of either of these giving them the right to avoid a claim.

In the case of Navigators and General v. Ringrose [1961] LL 415, a claim arose from the dismasting of a cruising catamaran some 30 miles south of Portland Bill on a cruise from Teignmouth to the Channel Islands. The yacht was insured under a dinghy policy for use 'whilst within the United Kingdom, ashore or afloat'. A steamer picked up the owner and his craft, and later submitted a claim for salvage. The insurers claimed that, since the incident occurred outside the insurance limits, they were not legally obliged to pay. The owner contended that the Channel Islands are part of the United Kingdom, and that, even if they are not, the policy covered a wide range of sea beyond the British mainland.

The Court of Appeal found that the Channel Islands were not part of the United Kingdom, and further that a spot 28 miles from shore was also not within the United Kingdom. Furthermore, even if the Channel Islands were within the UK, a voyage from one port to another of the UK would not mean that the waters between were part of the UK. The court therefore dismissed the owner's case, but recognised that whatever words are used to describe the cruising limits will give rise to anomalies.

Many dinghy and small craft policies restrict use to 'inland and coastal waters of the United Kingdom'. Coastal waters may be ten yards or ten miles offshore and, in the absence of any specific court ruling, there is an area of uncertainty in defining the precise extent of the cover. It is likely, however, that the Territorial Seas Act which defines areas within a notional 12 mile limit would be held to define coastal waters, while the Customs and Excise Management Act 1979 (Section 69) indicates the areas which may be regarded as coastal for the carriage of goods between places in the United Kingdom. For this purpose a passage between Liverpool and the Isle of Man is treated as coastal.

Most proposal forms allow the insured a choice of cruising ranges as follows:

- Non tidal
- Ten mile radius of moorings
- UK Coastal and Inland
- UK Inland and Coastal Waters including continental waters, Brest to Elbe limits

For skippers proposing to go offshore, it would be better to select the widest possible area; they should check with their insurers that a proposed cruise to Southern Ireland will be covered as it has been alleged on at least one occasion in recent times that item four above does not cover this area. Owners wishing to go further afield will need to make special arrangements, usually at an increased premium.

The owner must also take care over the dates that his yacht is to be in commission, and laid up. The longer the period in commission, the higher the premium will usually be, although there are now some underwriters who offer a flat rate irrespective of the length of lay-up period, if any. Since modern practice is to keep yachts in commission for even longer periods, to take advantage of the lower maintenance requirements of modern yachts, more effective and reliable forecasting and navigational systems, and better protective clothing, the penalty attached to a longer period in commission is likely to disappear altogether in due course.

Perils of the sea

The standard policy refers to 'perils of the seas'; this has been defined by the courts as: 'every accidental circumstance not the result of ordinary wear and tear, delay or act of the assured, happening in the course of navigation, and causing loss to the subject matter of the insurance'.

If, for example, a skin fitting has corroded and leaked, and the yacht has sunk as a consequence, this would not normally be a recoverable loss, any more than a motor insurance policy would cover the direct consequences of rust damage to a car.

Even so, the rejection of a claim by an underwriter on the ground that the part that failed was worn, weak or previously damaged, should be critically and logically examined. To carry this argument to an absurd conclusion, no damage would ever be payable since all damage is ultimately caused by some failure in some part of the yacht. The underwriter is required to (and usually does) apply the principle of fortuity realistically, having regard to the design of the yacht in question, and the age, size and strength of her spars and fittings.

Exclusion clause

Clause 10 of the standard policy states:

No claim shall be allowed in respect of:
i   outboard motors dropping off or falling overboard
ii   ship's boats having a maximum designed speed exceeding 17 knots, unless such boat is specially covered herein, and subject also to the conditions of the Speedboat Clause 19 below, or is on the parent vessel or laid up ashore

iii ship's boat not permanently marked with the name of the parent vessel

iv sails and protective covers split by the wind or blown away while set, unless in consequence of damage to the spars to which sails are bent, or occasioned by the vessel being stranded or in collision or contact with any external substance (ice included) other than water

v sails, masts, spars or standing and running rigging while the vessel is racing, unless the loss or damage is caused by the vessel being stranded, sunk, burnt, on fire or in collision or contact with any external substance (ice included) other than water

vi personal effects

vii consumable stores, fishing gear or moorings

viii sheathing, or repairs thereto, unless the loss or damage has been caused by the vessel being stranded, sunk, burnt, on fire or in collision or contact with any external substance (ice included) other than water

ix loss or expenditure incurred in remedying a fault in design or construction or any cost or expense incurred by reason of betterment or alteration in design or construction

x motor and connections (but not strut shaft or propeller) electrical equipment and batteries and connections, where the loss or damage has been caused by heavy weather, unless the loss or damage has been caused by the vessel being immersed, but this clause shall not exclude loss or damage caused by the vessel being stranded or in collision or contact with another vessel, pier or jetty.

Most of the above exclusions are self-explanatory, but 10.4 requires some explanation as the exclusion that is of most concern to the average owner. In the 1983 case of Webzell v. Raven (Unreported – Mayor & City of London Court) it was held that wind damage to a roller-furling headsail that had been left rigged (but furled) while the yacht was lying at her moorings was not payable under the policy.

In construing the words of the clause, the owner contended that the sail was not 'set' although it had been left rigged. The judge found that the words 'while set' applied only to sails that were 'blown away'; and that the exclusion for 'sails and protective covers split by the wind' did not rely on their being set at the time. Therefore the owner's claim failed. Despite this, most owners of roller furling headsails still leave them rigged throughout the year, in cheerful disregard of the fact that they are not insured.

Third party insurance

Collision with another vessel is only one of many forms of damage that a yacht may inflict on other persons or property. The standard wording for third party cover is widely drafted, and provides as follows: 'The underwriters agree to indemnify the Assured for any sum or sums which the Assured shall become legally liable to pay and shall pay, by reason of interest in the insured vessel and arising out of accidents during the currency of this insurance.' The clause also extends to the legal costs of the Assured, including representation at an inquest or a fatal accident hearing.

The question often arises as to the size of third party indemnity to be obtained. Many insurers limit the sum to £500 000, on the basis that most claims will in any event be subject to the limit of liability of the Merchant Shipping Acts. However other companies offer £1m or more on the grounds that personal injury awards in the English courts for serious injuries are already tending towards this figure. Also there are circumstances in which a Defendant may not be able to claim limitation of liability, including injury caused to a passenger or crew member of the vessel causing the injury; to cover against such circumstances the £1m level may seem to be a sensible precaution.

Duty to minimise loss

Clause 15.1 of the policy requires the Assured, in the case of a 'loss or misfortune' having occurred, to take all reasonable measures to prevent or minimise further loss or damage occurring. This would require him, for example, to take immediate steps to have the yacht recovered if she had dragged her anchor and had gone ashore with a risk of further damage, theft or vandalism. In the event of hull damage, he should take immediate steps to have 'first aid' repairs carried out where necessary in order to prevent the further ingress of water which would cause more extensive damage.

Theft

Clause 9.2.1.4 provides cover for theft of the entire vessel, or her boat(s), or outboard motor(s) provided it is securely locked to the vessel or her boat(s) by an anti-theft device in addition to the normal method of attachment. Also, following forcible entry to the vessel or place of storage or repair, theft of machinery including outboard motors, gear or equipment.

In a claim for stolen equipment, the requirement for 'forcible entry' means that propellers or outdrives unbolted and stolen from yachts laid up ashore will not be covered, while the terms 'gear and equipment' is limited to those items which would normally form part of the inventory of the boat when sold. This would include navigational equipment, charts, and perhaps binoculars, but would exclude cameras and personal effects which should be separately insured and declared on the proposal form.

Making a claim

After an incident causing damage to the insured yacht or a third party, or the possibility of a salvage claim, it is important to inform the insurers as soon as possible, even if it is not at the time certain that a claim need be made on the policy. In most cases this will mean advising the broker who will immediately notify the underwriter and send the Assured a claim form.

Where damage has left the yacht vulnerable to further damage or decay, the fact that the owner has notified the insurers does not of course exonerate him from taking immediate steps to prevent further problems arising, whether by having the yacht pulled out of the water or having an area of damage protected from attack by the elements. The rule in all such cases is that the owner must act as if uninsured and any further loss caused by a failure to do so will not be payable.

As much care should be taken in filling in the claim form as the proposal form, and a copy kept for future reference in case of dispute. The insurers will usually ask for at least one repair estimate to be attached.

Once a claim has been made, if physical damage has been done to the yacht, the underwriter will normally appoint a surveyor to inspect the damage and make recommendations for repairs. Although it is not unusual for a surveyor to try to do so, he is not authorised to give repair instructions to the boatyard; the yard is employed by the yacht owner and it is from the owner that any directions must come. The function of the surveyor is merely to advise the underwriter in his dealings with the owner. If the surveyor approves the claim and agrees the estimate for repairs, it is for the brokers, acting on the underwriter's instructions, to inform the owner and for the owner to give the go-ahead to the yard to carry out repairs. In all cases the owner should ensure that a full schedule of agreed works is prepared in advance, and insist that any additional items of work found to be necessary in the course of the repair should not be dealt with until inspected and approved by the underwriter's surveyor. Failure to obtain the surveyor's

June-Pamela is in a sorry state after being 'landed' during flooding in the Norfolk Broads. Once the owner has made a claim, the underwriter will appoint a surveyor to inspect the vessel and make recommendations for repairs.

approval will quite properly entitle the underwriter to refuse payment on any such extras.

As a point of principle, most underwriters will refuse to disclose the contents of a surveyor's report to the owner, whose only clue to the contents will be the underwriter's attitude to the claim. Since it is the surveyor's job to minimise the underwriter's liability, conflicts of opinion may arise as to what constitutes an adequate repair. Where there is a serious difference of opinion the owner may want to appoint his own surveyor to report on the damage and recommend the means of repair. Where this is done a compromise settlement will usually be possible but, if the dispute continues, his own surveyor's report will form the basis of his legal case against the underwriter.

Throughout the conduct of a claim, all communications between the Assured and the underwriter will be channelled through the broker (or with the claims department of an insurance company). It is important to remember that the broker acts for the Assured, and while he cannot of course fabricate evidence, or encourage the Assured to do so, he should be prepared to take a robust attitude with the underwriter if necessary, not just acting as a post box.

On completion of the repair work, the owner will normally be required to settle the bills himself, with the underwriter only issuing one single payment on seeing the receipted invoices and a certificate of satisfaction signed by the owner. Where the underwriter has appointed his own surveyor, he will be asked to report his own satisfaction independently to the underwriter.

Total loss

It may be that the damage to the yacht is so serious as to amount to an actual total loss or a constructive total loss. The former means complete destruction or deprivation; the latter arises when the yacht is reasonably abandoned because its loss appears inevitable or because repairs would cost so much that they would exceed its value when repaired. In such cases the Assured gets the option of treating the loss as total, subject to the insurers having the chance to recoup part of their payout by the salvage value.

In the case of a vessel that is stolen, or 'trapped' by hostilities, although Section 60 of the Marine Insurance Act requires recovery to be unlikely for a claim for constructive total loss to succeed, the courts have imposed a time limit in favour of the Assured, that recovery must be likely within a reasonable time. What constitutes a reasonable time in any case will depend on the facts. In *The Bamburi* [1982] 1 LL 312 a merchant ship became trapped in the Shatt-al-Arab waterway between Iran and Iraq during hostilities. Notice of abandonment was tendered by the Assured to the underwriters while the vessel was trapped, but was declined by the underwriters. One of the questions before the judge was whether the vessel could be considered a constructive total loss, the owners being unlikely to recover the vessel within a reasonable time. The judge found that a reasonable time in the circumstances would be 12 months from the date when notice of abandonment was given; and in this case it was unlikely that the owner could rescue the ship within that period. The Assured therefore succeeded in his claim.

Arbitration

Although some cases will inevitably finally involve specialist marine insurance lawyers and surveyors, it is always worthwhile following up alternative means of arbitration to have a claim settled before starting legal proceedings. Where a claim has been rejected on technical grounds it will often be worthwhile the Assured appointing a qualified surveyor not only to prepare a report, but also to negotiate on his behalf. In the case of a specialist small craft surveyor, the underwriter may well respect his opinion as much as that of the surveyor he himself has appointed, and a limited expenditure on non-legal professional fees at this stage may well be helpful in influencing the underwriter's response to a claim.

Where a claim is being mishandled by the broker or under-writer, or rejected on doubtful grounds, a reference to the Insurance Ombudsman (if the yacht is insured with a company) or to the Consumer Complaints Department at Lloyd's (if insured with a Lloyd's underwriter) will provide a form of free arbitration on the Assured's behalf.

CHAPTER TEN

SALVAGE

The law applying to salvage claims at sea differs enormously from the principles that govern the remainder of English law. The common law of the land recognises only two grounds of civil liability namely contract and tort. On land, if a person takes steps, whether at risk to himself or not, to protect or save another's life or property, he does not legally become entitled to any reward.

At sea the position is wholly different, and the law from ancient times has imposed on the owner of a vessel saved on the high seas an obligation to compensate the salvor. Furthermore, the Merchant Shipping Act 1894 Section 546 reinforces this rule by imposing a statutory obligation to pay a reasonable amount of salvage when claims are made for craft saved on or near the coasts of the United Kingdom.

The right to a reward is based on the principle that a person who has encountered a danger, and has expended work and labour to the benefit of another ship, should receive some remuneration. It is very much in the interests of public policy, and in the general interest of ships and marine commerce, that such rescue work should be undertaken. Indeed, unless a salvor could be sure of receiving a reasonable reward, there would be little incentive in putting one's own vessel and crew at risk to save another's property.

The main requirements for a successful salvage claim are as follows:

- The service must be carried out to a legally recognised subject of salvage; this is to say, to vessels, their gear, cargo or merchandise, or wreck, or freight at risk

- The salvor must act within the law
- The service must be voluntary and not under some pre-arranged contract
- The subject of the salvage service must be in danger
- The service must be successful
- The service must be performed in tidal waters

Before a rescuer can make a successful salvage claim, he must show that the property is maritime property. Not all property floating in tidal waters is maritime property, and it has been held in the Admiralty Court that an unmanned lightship, which was constructed and used solely for the purpose of an aid to navigation, cannot be the subject of a salvage claim. The same would be true if a high tide carried away a sailing club's launching trolley and it was later rescued, or if the club's racing buoys came adrift. The case of a floating object like a pontoon would probably be similar as a court would be unlikely to decide that it was used in navigation. The Civil Aviation Act 1982 provides that aircraft may be the subject of salvage claims, and if used in a rescue operation, may also be instrumental in making such a claim. In 1983 a Royal Navy Harrier jump jet which was too low in fuel to return to its carrier landed on the Spanish freighter *Alraigo* and the ship's owner and crew successfully claimed salvage.

Where a salvor finds a wreck or other maritime property, he is required by law to hand it over without delay to the Receiver of Wrecks. In practice this is usually the local Customs, or Coastguard Officer. There are criminal penalties for failing to hand over wreck, as there are for hiding, defacing, or taking it away. The Receiver can obtain a Magistrate's warrant to carry out a search of suspected premises.

When wreck, be it an unclaimed dinghy, sail covers, or any other ship's gear, comes into the possession of the Receiver, he is required to post a notice within 48 hours at the local Customs House, describing the property, and a further notice must go to Lloyd's of London. If the article is of low value, or is perishable, then it must be sold and the net proceeds retained for the owner.

It occasionally happens that a finder fails to hand over property to the Receiver of Wrecks, but contacts the owner direct and refuses to surrender the property unless paid a substantial sum by way of salvage. This usually amounts to criminal action, and not only will the finder be subject to prosecution, but he will also be liable to forfeit his right to a salvage reward.

The law of salvage only applies in the absence of a prior duty, on the part of the salvor, to come to the assistance of the ship or the property in question. This sort of duty could arise from a contract between the parties, or from an official duty on the part of the salvor. Where a duty exists, the service is not voluntary, and the law of salvage, which is an emergency law outside the law of contract or provision of a public service, does not apply.

In most circumstances the crew of a vessel are not entitled to make any salvage claim in respect of the ship they are on since their contractual duties involve carrying out all the acts required to navigate the vessel safely, to keep her from danger, and to take steps to remove her from any danger that may arise.

In exceptional circumstances the crew may earn an award, but only after they have abandoned ship on the orders of the master in the honest belief that the ship was sinking and there was no likelihood of re-boarding. In the case of the *San Demetrio* which was set on fire by a German warship while in an Atlantic convoy in 1941, the crew abandoned ship in the fear that the ship would explode. Two days later the occupants of one of the lifeboats, which was manned by the Second Officer and 14 others, re-boarded the ship, put out the fires, restarted the engines, and sailed the ship to a safe haven. A salvage award was made in their favour. There is no record of any such occurrence involving a pleasure yacht.

Where a vessel has called for a tow, and a fee for the tow has been agreed, that is an agreement that is contractually binding on both parties, and the tug or towing vessel has to perform its obligations. This involves meeting any of the normally expected problems associated with towing with reasonable care, skill, and promptitude.

However, in the course of the tow an accident may make the towage contract impossible in the way the parties had envisaged. In those circumstances the contract will be suspended, and if the towing vessel continues to render assistance, that may constitute an act of salvage. This case may arise if a vessel is being towed under contract and, because of deteriorating weather, it becomes in danger through no fault of the tug. Many yachts are particularly difficult to tow in heavy seas. The tug may then, at law, be released from the contract and become free to provide a salvage service. If however the yacht owner could show that lack of skill or proper equipment on the part of the tug materially contributed to the danger, then the owner or crew of the tug will not be entitled to a salvage award.

More likely is the claim that an agreed tow was in fact a salvage service. In the case of the *Eileen Siocht* (1948) 82 LL 128, the vessels concerned were a 101-ton motor yacht, a pilot cutter, and a 4-ton motor launch. The yacht had been on passage from Hamble to Poole when she called for a pilot who, when he boarded, was told the engines were running badly. In the entrance to Poole Harbour the engines broke down completely. A passing motor launch and the pilot cutter took a tow-line each and towed her into the harbour;

once inside, the pilot cutter came alongside for a tow to Poole Town Quay. When a claim was made for salvage this was rejected by the court on the grounds that the motor yacht could have safely anchored while repairs were effected, and was therefore not in a position of danger. The court held that although the salvage claim failed, the Plaintiffs were entitled to a fee for the work done in towing the yacht to harbour.

Where property is saved by the actions of a public servant, such as a coastguard or harbour master, a salvage award will only be made if the service is outside the normal scope of his official duties. Where the officers or crew of a Royal Navy ship wish to claim for salvage, the written consent of the Ministry of Defence is required before any legal steps may be taken.

Where a salvage service is performed by a National Lifeboat Institution vessel, although it is the policy of the RNLI not to make salvage claims, it is open to the crew of the lifeboat to do so. With few exceptions the RNLI does not employ the crews who act as

The Arun class lifeboat RNLB Tony Vandervell *on service to the yacht* Sandpiper *off Weymouth in August 1992. Although the RNLI do not make salvage claims or towing charges, the lifeboat crew are permitted to do so with the RNLI recovering its costs against the salvage fees payable.*

volunteers, being rewarded on a modest scale whenever they go out on a service and provided they make no claim for salvage.

The RNLI permits its crews to use their vessels for salvage purposes provided that no other suitable craft are in the vicinity and provided that the lifeboat is not immediately required for other duties. If a salvage award is made, the RNLI will claim against the crew the costs of launching, hauling up, and rehousing the lifeboat, the costs of fuel and stores used, and the costs of any repairs or replacements.

Since any salvage award is payable out of the salved property, the salvor is not entitled to any reward unless he was successful; hence the expression 'no cure – no pay'. Difficulties can arise in cases where several sets of salvors have taken part in salvage work. It may be doubtful whether the first set of salvors to assist the vessel actually achieved anything in helping her. In the case of SS *Melanie* [1925] AC 246 the Court of Appeal stated that: 'Success is necessary for a salvage award. Contributions to that success ... give a title to salvage reward. Services, however meritorious, which do not contribute to the ultimate success, do not give a title to salvage reward.' By the same token, services which rescue a vessel from one danger but end by leaving her in a position of as great or nearly as great danger of another kind, are held not to contribute to the ultimate success and do not entitle to a salvage reward. In considering these questions, wherever the service is meritorious, the court has lent towards supporting a claim for salvage.

The principle that a salvage service must be performed in tidal waters was reaffirmed in the case of the *Goring* [1988] 1 LL 397. This case concerned a Thames passenger launch, moored near Reading Bridge, which broke free of her moorings during the night and was saved from drifting downstream by other boat owners. The salvors claimed that the Admiralty Court Act 1840 abolished the old rule that salvage could be claimed only on the High Seas, since Section 6 of the Act extended the jurisdiction of the Admiralty Court to claims for services 'within the body of a county'. It was argued that the words 'within the body of a county' were wide enough to include non-tidal inland waters navigable by ships, and that the Act had extended the scope of salvage law. However the House of Lords held that the terms of Section 546 of the Merchant Shipping Act 1894, limiting payment of salvage to cases arising 'at any place on or near the coasts of the United Kingdom, or any tidal water' should be followed, and that the purpose of the 1840 Act was to clarify the jurisdictional area of the Admiralty Court rather than extend the scope of the law administered by that court.

Whether a salvage claim can be made for a rescue within a harbour authority's jurisdiction was considered in the case of the

Powstaniec Wielkopolski [1989] 1 LL 58. In that case the ship was attempting to dock in high winds at Gravesend which is well within the jurisdiction of the Port of London Authority. Additional tugs had to come to the aid of the ship as control was lost, and eventually she was safely docked. In denying the salvage claim, the owners relied on the definition of 'tidal water' in the 1894 Act as being 'any part of the sea and any part of a river within the ebb and flow of the tide at ordinary spring tides, and not being a harbour', the definition of a harbour being ('unless the context otherwise requires') any 'harbour property so called, whether natural or artificial, estuaries, navigable rivers, piers, jetties, and other works in or at which ships can obtain shelter, or ship or unship goods or passengers'.

The court held however that the River Thames at Gravesend could not properly be called a harbour, as it was not a harbour in the ordinary and natural meaning of the word. The claim for salvage was therefore successful.

The Merchant Shipping Act 1988 finally cleared up this point with a further statutory definition, by which Section 546 of the 1894 Act was amended to define 'tidal water' as 'any waters within the ebb and flow of the tide at ordinary spring tides or the waters of any dock which is directly or (by means of one or more other docks) indirectly connected with any such waters'. Thus any salvage service either outside or inside a harbour or dock can now give rise to a claim.

Salvor's lien

Where a salvage service has been successfully carried out, the salvors will not normally be entitled to retain any property in their possession as they will automatically have a maritime lien over it. This gives the right to arrest the ship or property even if it subsequently changes hands, or the right to arrest a sister ship (ie a vessel in the same ownership) in order to enforce the salvors' claim for a salvage award.

In practice, however, there can often be a problem enforcing the lien, and the standard 'Lloyd's Open Form' salvage agreement, often used between parties, by agreement, in an emergency situation, entitles the salvor to ask for security to be provided to Lloyd's before the vessel leaves the jurisdiction of the British courts. Apart from having a claim against the ship, the salvors also have a personal claim against the owner which can also be pursued if necessary through the Admiralty Court.

The salvage award

Once the right to a salvage award has been decided on by the court, the question arises as to the size of the award. In making its assessment the court will look to the degree of risk involved, the length of time the service took, the number of people engaged, the relative values of the salved property and the salving vessel, the degree of danger from which the salved vessel was rescued, and the skill and labour employed by the rescuers. In addition, the court will take into account whether the salvor was a professional or amateur and, in the case of a professional salvor using a vessel specifically built and used for salvage services, will usually make a higher award.

Since the amount of the award is very much dependent on the exact details of each case, it is important for the skipper and crew of a yacht in circumstances that might lead to a salvage claim to take a careful note of all the circumstances, to show themselves as much as possible in control of the situation (eg by using their own gear) and take all reasonable steps to see that corroboration of their case (in the form of weather reports, charts with positions marked, and a well kept log) is available in the case of a dispute arising.

Since most yacht insurance policies cover salvage claims, the yacht owner's best course of action when faced with a possible salvage claim will be to inform the insurers and allow them to handle the situation. Indeed the insurance policy will usually require immediate written notice of any accident or any potential claim, and lay down that no negotiations, payments, settlements, admission or repudiation of any claim is given or made without the written consent of the insurers.

So far as the likely amount of a salvage award made by the courts is concerned, the only guidance available is reference to previously decided cases. In the case of *Ocean Hound* (1950) 84 LL 5, a 72 foot twin screw motor yacht went aground near Dungeness on a shingle bank, close to an old wreck and old sea defence works. The Dungeness Lifeboat, with ten crew, came to her assistance and, at her request, came alongside to refloat her. After ten minutes at full power she succeeded in pulling her off the bank and towed her out into deeper water. The value of the salved yacht was £1500, and the whole service took about $1^1/2$ hours. The salvors argued that the yacht would have damaged her bottom and screws at low water and that on the next high water would have been driven further ashore, probably fouling the sea defence works. They had incurred total expenses of £36. The court accepted that the weather might well have deteriorated and that the yacht was rescued from a position of considerable potential, if not actual, danger. The services rendered were easy for an experienced crew, but the award should be set high enough to provide a reasonable incentive to salvage property from danger. An award of £150, plus the expenses of £36, was made, to be divided equally between the ten crew.

In another case involving a lifeboat, the *Guernsey Coast* (1950) 83 LL 483 had received short but useful advice as to where to find deeper water when, in bad weather, she was bumping and dragging on Margate Sand. The judge awarded £250 on a salved value of £84 000.

In the case of the old 12 metre racing yacht *Evaine* [1966] 2 LL 413, the court awarded £750 on a salved value of £3000 to the crew of a fishing boat for going alongside and successfully fighting a fire after the yacht had been abandoned by her crew. The crew undertaking the salvage faced a very real risk of explosion in the circumstances which the court held justified the award of 25%.

An interesting case involving a salvage attempt that went wrong was the *St Blane* [1974] 1 LL 557. The steamship *St Blane* went to assist a yacht, the *Ariadne*, in distress in heavy weather in the Irish Sea. The yacht's owner, his wife and two sons were taken aboard the ship and the yacht itself was eventually secured alongside the ship. However the yacht began to sustain damage from the ship's hull, whereupon the master unsecured her and the yacht promptly sank. The yacht owner sued the ship's owner for the loss of his craft, alleging negligence in that the master of the ship had collided with the yacht whilst manoeuvring, and had secured her alongside longer than necessary. The yacht owner claimed that the sinking was the direct consequence of that negligence. The *St Blane*'s owners denied these allegations, and claimed that the yacht owner himself had been negligent.

The court held that the master of the ship had not acted unreasonably in his initial making fast of the yacht, and that the yacht owner had failed to establish that the collision with the yacht was due to the negligent handling of the ship. Moreover, the ship's master was not a professional salvor, and could only, in performing the operation, work in the time-honoured principle of 'trial and error'.

If the court is called upon to apportion the salvage award between the owner, master and crew of the sailing vessel, it must do (under Section 556 of the Merchant Shipping Act 1894), 'in such manner as it thinks just', unless this is barred by a valid agreement. The court will have to assess the level of risk to the salving vessel and compensate the owner according to whether the salvage was attributable mainly to the salving vessel and its equipment or to the skill of the master and crew. Since towing has become the most frequent form of salvage service, the courts will normally apportion a larger amount to the owners. The owners might be awarded three-quarters of the reward, in the case of a specialist tug performing a rescue, or perhaps two-thirds where, for example, a non-specialist fishing vessel performs the salvage.

In the case of the *Ben Gairn* [1979] 1 LL 410, a trawler towed another for 16 miles at night in rough seas. There was some danger to the salving vessel, and the master carried a heavy responsibility. The salved vessel was valued at £55 000. An award of £5400 was made, apportioned two-thirds to the owners and one-third to the crew. Of the crew's share, the master was awarded £650, the mate £250, and the remaining £900 was shared between the 9 crew.

Salvage agreements

Most surveyor services performed by professional salvors are given under the terms of the Lloyd's standard Form of Salvage Agreement. This is known as the Lloyd's Open Form as it leaves 'open' the amount of salvage reward which is later decided upon by an arbitrator. This is clearly preferable to the parties having to agree, often under life-threatening conditions, on the exact terms under which the salvor will operate. A salvage contract must be distinguished from a towage contract, where for example a tug is offered on a daily rate for simply towing. Here the tug owner would be paid for any work done, even if the ship sinks. Where a salvage agreement does fix a price, it will usually be a lump sum or a daily rate rather than a percentage of the salved value.

In a salvage agreement the services must be given on a 'no cure – no pay' basis. Only in such a case does the salvor acquire a maritime lien, and if any sum is agreed it will be paid out of the salved value. If a salvor fails to perform the exact service he has agreed under the 'no cure – no pay' contract, he may still be entitled to claim an amount under the general law of salvage.

The Lloyd's Open Form, which dates back over 100 years, is an agreement for arbitration which removes disputes about the exact sum payable to the jurisdiction of an arbitrator appointed by Lloyd's. The effect of this agreement is to give the salvor an undisputed right to a salvage award. It would be very difficult for the owner of a yacht to claim later that the agreement was for towage and not salvage. A shortened version of the Lloyd's Open Form suitable for the salvage of a yacht is reprinted in Appendix 5.

Life salvage

Under Section 6 of the Maritime Conventions Act 1911, every master of a British ship (and that term includes yachts of any size, even

A submerged yacht in Weymouth harbour being salvaged with the aid of lifting bags. When entering into any salvage agreement, make sure that the services are given on a 'no cure – no pay' basis.

down to a small sailing dinghy) is under a duty 'so far as he can, without serious danger to his vessel, her crew, and passengers (if any) to render assistance to every person (even enemies in wartime) who is found at sea in danger of being lost'. However, a salvor who rescues the crew or passengers of a vessel, and also salves either the vessel or part of its cargo, may add to his salvage claim a further claim for saving those lives. Such a claim can only be made if there is salvage of some material (eg ship or cargo) in addition to the lives, which can provide the means of paying the claim.

CHAPTER ELEVEN

HARBOUR LAW

Although the free public right of navigation on tidal waters takes precedence over the rights of the fundus (sea bed) owners, the law has always recognised that, if a safe haven is created by the provision of harbour works, the person who did this could legally demand a fee from whoever benefited from his work.

For the purposes of the Merchant Shipping Acts, Section 742 of the 1894 Act defines 'harbour' as including 'harbours, properly so called, whether natural or artificial, estuaries, navigable rivers, piers, jetties, and other works in or at which ships can obtain shelter, or ship and unship goods or passengers'. The Harbours Act 1964 defines a harbour authority for the purposes of that Act as 'any person in whom are vested ... powers or duties of improving, maintaining or managing a harbour'.

Harbour administrations today are usually based on a private Act of Parliament which covers the harbour in question and which will also normally incorporate parts of the Harbours, Docks and Piers Clauses Act 1847. The particular powers of any harbour authority depend on the exact terms of its own private legislation. It will usually be the case that the principal Act will deal with the appointment of the harbour Trustees, and the vesting in them of the harbour undertaking. It will set out the harbour limits, and give the Trustees extensive powers to maintain the harbour and its equipment. It will prohibit any building without the Trustees' consent, make provision for light signals, buoyage and life saving equipment, and deal with dues on vessels, passengers and goods, and the exemptions from such dues, and will define the Harbour Masters' powers over vessels. It will also give powers to make byelaws for specific matters which will be in addition to the powers contained in the 1847 Act, these being inadequate for modern conditions and requirements.

For historical reasons ports may be managed in a number of ways under a variety of different constitutions. The majority of small ports in the country are trust ports, run by a board of commissioners or trustees either appointed by parties nominated in each harbour's own Act, or by other existing trustees. Other ports are managed by local authorities, often by a sub-committee of the local Council, or other authorities; thus the National Rivers Authority is responsible for the Harbour of Rye, and the Hampshire County Council for the Hamble River. An increasing number of harbours are privately owned. The British Transport Docks Board was privatised in 1982 to become Associated British Ports, running such important areas in Southampton and the Humber ports, while the 1991 Ports Act provides for the compulsory privatisation of trust ports with an annual turnover in excess of £5m. There are a number of small privately owned harbours, such as Portishead Dock, Bembridge and the River Crouch, all of which have their own legislation, while harbours such as the River Beaulieu and Newtown Creek, also privately owned, enjoy some characteristics of a harbour (including the right to charge visitors in some cases) but without any private Act of Parliament specifying those rights. A fast-shrinking category of harbour are the Naval Dockyards, each managed by a Queen's Harbour Master on behalf of the Ministry of Defence.

Functions of harbour authorities

The main functions of harbour authorities, which are discussed below in greater detail, are as follows:

1 Regulating the activities of other persons at the harbour including particularly the movement and berthing of ships in the harbour by means of directions and byelaws, licensing dredging, and the construction of works in the harbour by other persons

2 The provision and maintenance of harbour facilities such as sea walls, quays, wharves, moorings etc

3 Conservancy functions, including lighting and buoying the harbour, the removal of wrecks and other obstructions, and maintenance dredging and cleaning up pollution

4 The carrying out of harbour operations including cargo and passenger handling

5 The provision of pilotage services

The powers granted to a harbour authority by Parliament are in most cases conferred for the purpose of providing a public service. The intention of Parliament is expressed most clearly in Section 33 of the Harbours, Docks and Piers Clauses Act 1847 which provides that 'upon payment of the rates made payable by this ... Act, and subject to the other provisions thereof, the harbour, dock and pier shall be open to all persons for the shipping and unshipping of goods and the embarking and landing of passengers'. The right of the public to enter any harbour applies as much to pleasure craft as to commercial or fishing craft, and only the Queen's Harbour Masters at Naval Dockyards have the authority to refuse entry to a harbour; elsewhere in the country all harbours must be kept open to the public to bring in whatever craft they wish (so long as they are not in a dangerous condition or carrying a dangerous cargo) subject only to the harbour being physically capable of accommodating them.

Powers to regulate activities

From the pleasure boat owner's point of view the most important power vested in the Harbour Master is the power to give directions, and to dictate where a boat should go or not go. This power derives from Section 52 of the 1847 Act which authorises the Harbour Master to give directions:

'for regulating the time at which and the manner in which any vessel shall enter into, go out of, or lie in or at the harbour, dock or pier, and within the prescribed limits, if any, and its position, mooring or unmooring, placing and remooring, whilst therein'.

Section 53 of the Act provides that:

'The master of every vessel within the harbour ... shall regulate such vessel according to the directions of the Harbour Master, made in conformity with this and the special (ie the harbour's private) Act; and any master who, after notice of any such direction by the Harbour Master served upon him, shall not (comply) shall be liable to a penalty.'

The scope of a Harbour Master's powers was considered in the case of the *Guelder Rose* [1927] 136 LT 226. The Fowey Harbour Master had given a direction that between sunset and sunrise certain vessels should be limited to three knots, should only anchor in a specified place, should not at any time proceed beyond a certain point without the sanction of the Harbour Master, and should not

The Harbour Master's word is final!

at any time move within the harbour without his prior consent. This direction was held by the High Court to be *ultra vires* (ie the Harbour Master was acting in excess of his authority, or beyond his powers). In his judgment Lord Aiken said:

'That does not appear to me to be in the least a matter for which jurisdiction was given to the Harbour Master. Speaking generally, it appears to me that the object of Section 52 is fairly obvious. The Harbour Master is the person who controls the movements of the particular vessels when they are within the port ... and his powers are given to him for the purpose of giving specific directions to specific ships for specific movements.'

The same point was considered by the High Court in the case of Pearn v. Sargent [1973] 2 AC 141. The Harbour Master at Looe had issued a direction that no vessel should move anywhere within the harbour while a regatta was in progress. This regatta itself was only taking place at the seaward end of the harbour, and the direction was ignored by the commercial operator of pleasure craft. The court held that the direction was *ultra vires*. In the words of Lord Widgery

'The function of the Harbour Master under Section 52 is to regulate the traffic; after all it is a public harbour and the public have a right to be there, and it is not the Harbour Master's function, as such, to keep them out. His function is to control and regulate them rather like a traffic policeman regulating the traffic. Of course there will be cases when he has to go beyond these simple functions; of course there may be cases where necessity arises and he has to impose wider prohibitions for a particular time, but when that happens it is for consideration whether the directions he has given are reasonable for the emergency or circumstances which prompted them.'

Following the *Guelder Rose* and Pearn v. Sargent cases a number of harbour authorities have extended their powers by adding a clause to their own private Act to the effect that Section 52 of the 1847 Act, as incorporated in their own enabling Act:

a shall extend to empower the Harbour Master to give directions prohibiting the mooring of vessels in any particular part or parts of the harbour; and

b shall not be construed to require the Harbour Master in emergency to give particular directions in the case of every vessel in respect of which it is desired to exercise any of the powers of that section, but in pursuance of that section for all or any of the purposes thereof the Harbour Master shall be entitled in emergency to give general directions applicable to all vessels or to particular classes of vessels.

The extent of a Harbour Master's power to give general directions was considered in 1982 when a proposal by a shipping company to establish a permanent gas storage and trans-shipment facility in the Solent was being considered by the Southampton Harbour Authority. The scheme would have involved a liquefied petroleum gas tanker of over 30 000 tons on a permanent mooring 1000 yards north of Old Castle Point at Cowes. During loading or offloading operations, a 500 yard security radius was to be imposed to reduce the risk of explosion, at the insistence of the vessel's insurers. The harbour authority received the advice that although the permanent mooring of the gas tanker might be within their powers, the imposition of a safety radius on a regular basis in an area that was well-established as a cruising and racing area for recreational craft would be an unreasonable use of the authority's powers to give directions to traffic, and as such would be legally unenforceable. Partly for legal reasons, and partly because of the huge public outcry over the proposal, the plan was later withdrawn.

As the busiest recreational and commercial harbour area in western Europe, Southampton was again the subject of legal argument over a proposal in 1987 to impose a no-go zone on pleasure craft under 20 metres from the area to the north and west of the Brambles Bank. The Harbour Master wished to exclude small craft from the deep water channel in this area to help the passage of large commercial vessels around this difficult turn. The harbour authority was advised that a permanent exclusion of this sort was unreasonable and therefore unenforceable. An alternative proposal that the exclusion zone should only be operative when a large vessel was in the vicinity proved to be more acceptable, and in 1992 this was further amended to a requirement for small craft not to pass within 1000 metres of the bow of a large vessel (over 150 metres in length).

The authority to give general directions is thus a useful management power for a Harbour Master, but as in all cases of public jurisdiction, there is an over-riding legal requirement that such powers should be exercised reasonably, and any aggrieved person can apply to the High Court at any time for a declaration that an act or threatened act is unlawful.

Further controls on vessel movements and activities can be imposed by means of permanent byelaws, provided the relevant Harbour Act contains such provisions for byelaws to be made. Matters such as speed limits, reporting requirements, prohibiting of waterskiing or using personal watercraft (Jet-skis, wet bikes etc), limiting of windsurfing to areas outside the main shipping channels, and restrictions on anchoring in the fairway are all examples of the sort of long-term controls that may be valid for many years, and which are not suitable to be dealt with by means of general directions. Most harbours impose a byelaw requirement that no regatta, rally or organised gathering of yachts may take place without at least 14 days' prior notice to the Harbour Master. Occasionally attempts by harbour authorities are made to extend this by new byelaws requiring the consent of the Harbour Master in advance. In practice this goes beyond what is necessary for the safe management of the harbour and objections of the Department of Transport are usually successful on the grounds that a 'prior notice' provision is all that is required.

Provision and maintenance of harbour facilities

Although many harbour authorities provide long-term mooring facilities for pleasure craft in addition to short-term berthing and wharfage for commercial craft, there is in most cases no compulsion for them to do so. The free public right of navigation includes the right of incidental anchoring, for reasonable periods of time, to embark or disembark passengers and crew, to wait for the tide, or simply to take a rest. This principle applies as much to tidal waters within a harbour area as elsewhere, although in this case the harbour authority will be entitled to levy harbour dues. Thus any pleasure yacht entering a harbour is entitled to anchor wherever it wishes provided that no obstruction to navigation is created, and that no local byelaws or Harbour Master's general directions are broken. In most harbours there are areas set aside for visitors to anchor, and other areas set aside for long-term moorings.

The provision of pleasure craft moorings by harbour authorities originated as a means of ensuring good order and discipline in mooring areas rather than a means of raising substantial revenue. For a harbour authority to lay moorings for rent to the public it is not sufficient for it simply to have the power to license moorings; it must also either own or lease the fundus on or in which the ground tackle is to be laid. In most cases the fundus will be in the ownership of one of the major public landlords, such as the Crown Estate Commissioners, the Duchy of Cornwall, or the Duchy of Lancaster.

Harbour authority moorings

Moorings can be made available by harbour authorities either as an entire package, including the provision and maintenance of the ground tackle, riser, and mooring buoy (and even in some cases a ferry service from the public landing), or as the provision of a mooring site on which the boat owner must provide his own tackle. In the latter case it is the policy of the Crown Estate Commissioners, when leasing a mooring area to a harbour authority, local authority, or some other non-profit making provider of mooring plots, that the rent charged to the individual boat owner should not be marked up by more than 25% of the rent charged by the Crown Estate. This simple formula is designed to prevent the authorities from profiteering from the letting of moorings at times when demand exceeds supply. In 1984 the Property Services Agency, managing large areas of fundus on behalf of the Ministry of Defence within the Plymouth Dockyard area, proposed a scheme whereby moorings would be let out by tender to the highest bidders. The public outcry caused by this proposal (which would have effectively forced many of the less well-off local people with small craft off the water altogether) led the Duchy of Cornwall, the ultimate landlord of the area, to persuade the PSA to abandon the scheme.

The rents charged by the major public landlords to non-profit making bodies have tended to be relatively modest, although in the late 1980s and early 1990s there were substantial increases in some south coast harbours. At Lymington the annual rental was increased in 1990 from £3000 per annum to over £100 000 for the 700 or so moorings under the control of the harbour commissioners. With a limited number of mooring areas available in the more popular yachting centres, and a steadily increasing boat owning population, it is inevitable that mooring prices will increase in future years unless some formal control mechanism can be imposed and agreed.

Where a harbour authority supplies and maintains mooring tackle for use by yacht owners, it has a legal duty to exercise reasonable care and skill in laying and maintaining moorings.

In the case of the *Quercus* [1943] P 96, a 7 ton yacht was moored in Torquay Harbour. The Defendants were the local Council who owned the mooring and had hired it out to the yacht owner. During a gale, when the wind and tide in the harbour were high, but not abnormally so, the mooring parted and the yacht became a total loss. The chain which broke had a diameter of $3/4$ inch, with 9-inch links. The mooring parted as a result of kinking as the mooring swivel had seized up owing to rust and marine growth. The court held that, since the Defendants had supplied the tackle, they were liable for its failure unless they could prove that they had not been negligent in maintaining it. The court held that a quick inspection once a year by a diver who could not see small fractures or distortions of the links was inadequate. The diver should have unshackled the chain and swivel and given it a proper examination on the deck of the boat. The Defendants were found liable for negligence. This case throws a high duty of care on mooring owners, and in particular on clubs that provide moorings for members and visitors.

Harbour dues

Under the terms of the Harbours Act 1964, a harbour authority is entitled to impose such charges by way of 'ship, passenger, and goods dues' as it thinks fit subject to a right of appeal by users to the Secretary of State for Transport. The definition of ship, passenger and goods dues in the Act includes the following:

> 'Charges in respect of any ship for entering, using or leaving the harbour, including charges made on the ship for marking or lighting the harbour.'

In addition to the statutory power to levy dues, a harbour authority has the implied power to charge for services which it is authorised to provide, subject to the proviso that such charges must be reasonable.

Section 31 of the Harbour Act provides for written objections to be made to the Secretary of State for Transport as respects ship, passenger and goods dues imposed by a harbour authority at their harbour. Any objector must be a person having substantial interests in the question, or a body representing a number of such persons. Objections may be made on any of the following grounds:

- That the charge ought not to be imposed at all
- That the charge ought to be imposed at a lower rate
- That, according to the circumstances of the case, ships, passengers or goods of a class specified in the objection ought to be excluded or reduced from the scope of the charge either generally or in circumstances so specified.

Where objections are made, the Secretary of State will hold an enquiry, as a result of which he may approve the charge, or give directions to the harbour authority to reduce or abolish the charge or otherwise satisfy the objection.

In 1982 the Weymouth and Portland Council introduced a substantial charge on vessels (£70 per double transit) for the raising and lowering of the lifting bridge, it being the first time that such a charge had been made on any of the many lifting and swing bridges over tidal waters in the country. The inspector appointed to hear the public enquiry heard evidence of the charges (or lack of them) at all other bridges in the country, including Tower Bridge in London, and subsequently the Secretary of State directed the local authority to abandon the charge.

Another question that often arises is whether a mooring charge is a ship due, and therefore subject to the Section 31 objection procedure. Mooring charges are either charges made for the use of a mooring provided by the authority in a harbour, or a charge made by the harbour authority for the grant to a person of a licence to lay and maintain his own mooring in the harbour. So far as the latter is concerned, it is likely that such a charge is not made 'in respect of any ship for entering, using, or leaving the harbour', although this has never been tested in court. So far as charges for the use of moorings is concerned, it is argued that where the moorings could be said to form part of the infrastructure of the harbour, in the same way as the docks and wharves of the harbour, it is a charge for a ship using the harbour and therefore subject to the Section 31 procedure. This matter was considered in 1990 in the case of a Section 31 objection to harbour and mooring dues in the Hamble River, where it was alleged that an excessive surplus, over and above that required to manage the harbour properly, was being made, and transferred to subsidise other activities of the Hampshire County Council. The Authority took the view that mooring charges were, unlike harbour dues, purely at their discretion, and not subject to review by the Secretary of State for Transport. The view of the objectors was that the Harbour Revision Order from which the Authority derived its powers specifically referred to the moorings and mooring piles as part of the harbour undertaking, which in the context of the main business of the Hamble River as a pleasure yacht harbour, clearly implied that the moorings formed part of the harbour infrastructure, and therefore mooring charges were subject to the Section 31 procedure. Sadly the parties reached a compromise agreement, and the lawyers were denied the opportunity of arguing and resolving the matter.

Harbour dues in natural harbours

Although in most cases the right to charge for use of a harbour is based on statute, in some harbours yacht owners are asked to pay a fee where nothing in the way of protective works or dredging has been provided, and no statutory authority exists. A claim of this sort cannot be based on ownership of the foreshore. A foreshore or fundus owner cannot claim a right, simply by that ownership, to charge for anchoring in his soil. The right of navigation takes precedence over his property right, and anchoring is part of the right of navigation. If he has placed moorings or other facilities he can charge for these, because the use of such facilities is not an exercise of the right of navigation.

A right to claim harbour tolls at a non-statutory harbour can however be founded on custom if the owner has provided some structure or service. In the case of a natural harbour, where there are no seawalls or piers, or other artificial works, and no duty to repair or dredge, the question whether tolls can properly be charged for use of it depends on whether or not the area over which such a right may be asserted would be held to be legally a 'port'. If not, charges may not be made if no benefit is provided. The owner of a natural inlet which is not a port cannot demand fees from yachts that anchor there for shelter or convenience.

This raises the question as to what is a port. If there is evidence that fees have been levied there for many years, and that navigation aids and any other facilities have been provided, then it will probably be held to be a port, and fees may properly be charged.

In the case of Gann v. Free Fishers of Whitstable [1864] 11 HLC 192, anchor dues were claimed for a natural roadstead though there was no maintenance by the owners. The House of Lords dismissed the owners' claim to dues on the ground that the vessel had used their fundus for anchoring. In the case of Foreman v. Free Fishers of Whitstable [1869] LR 4HL 266, a very different approach was taken, since dues had been paid for many years, and they provided navigation aids, the area was a port and they were entitled to port dues on vessels anchoring in the area. The House of Lords upheld their claim, but stressed the importance of the owners being able to prove that dues had been levied since time immemorial.

Light dues

Although most buoys and lights within harbour areas are provided and maintained by the local harbour authority, Trinity House remain responsible for the majority of navigation aids around the remainder of the coast.

Trinity House was granted its first Charter by Henry VIII and one of its main tasks was to reduce the systematic wrecking and pillage of ships which was rife in those days. In the reign of Elizabeth I it was given, by statute, rights to erect and maintain 'beacons, marks, and signs of the sea', and became responsible for the provision of skilled pilots in certain waters, a service it still maintains in the English Channel and approaches to the Thames.

Light dues are payments made by ships for the maintenance of navigation aids. Certain small vessels, together with HM ships and empty freighters, are exempted, but otherwise all vessels pay on their net registered tonnage (or Thames Measurement Tonnage if not registered on the Part I Register). Pleasure yachts under 20 tons are exempted from the payment of light dues, largely on the grounds that there is no equitable and economical means by which they can be charged. The amount to be collected would be so low that the creation of a scheme of compulsory registration (as recommended by the British Ports Federation in 1990) would have resulted in more than half the proceeds of an annual registration charge being spent in setting up, maintaining and enforcing the register. The Government has been under pressure for many years to abolish light dues and follow the practice in nearly every maritime nation in the world and to pay for navigation aids out of general taxation.

Pilotage

Historically, pilotage has always been the responsibility of the pilotage authorities, of which Trinity House was the largest with responsibility for 40 out of the 90 pilotage districts around the country. The most important function of the authorities was the licensing of pilots for the district and the granting of pilotage certificates to Masters and First Mates to exempt them from carrying pilots in certain areas. The pilotage authorities were also responsible for the making and enforcement of pilotage byelaws, the making of pilotage charges, and the approval and licensing of pilots' boats.

Since the Pilotage Act 1987, responsibility for this function has largely moved to the harbour authorities, with some authorities entering into joint arrangements with other harbours in the same former pilotage district. Section 2 of the 1987 Act requires each relevant harbour authority to keep under consideration what pilotage services (if any) need to be provided to secure the safety of ships navigating in, or in the approaches to, their harbour and whether, in the interests of safety, pilotage should be compulsory in any part of that harbour or its approaches. If so, the authority must consider for what ships and in which circumstances pilotage is necessary, and what services should be provided. If the harbour authority sees a need for pilotage services over a wider area than its own harbour limits, it may apply for an order under Section 1 of the Act to extend its pilotage area without the need to extend its harbour limits.

So far as the pilotage of yachts and other small craft is concerned, there is a general statutory exemption for craft under 20 metres in length. Above that size it is for each harbour authority to decide at what level pilotage should be compulsory and to promote appropriate byelaws to enforce that. In practice there are few harbour authorities that enforce compulsory pilotage on yachts under 24 metres in length; in most cases the limit is very much higher than that.

Division of control between skipper and pilot

Prior to the Pilotage Act 1913 the owner or Master of a ship being navigated under compulsory pilotage was not answerable for any loss or damage caused by the fault of a compulsory pilot.

The 1913 Act changed the law by making the ship owner responsible for any loss or damage 'caused' by the vessel or by any fault of the navigation of the vessel, whether pilotage was compulsory or not. Consequently, since the ship owner had to pay the cost of any damage, the question as to who was actually responsible became academic. However, since 1988 most pilots have changed from being self-employed to being employees of harbour authorities, and accordingly ship owners who are primarily liable under the 1913 Act may be able to look to the harbour authorities as the pilots' employers, under the principle of vicarious liability, although no such case had come to court at the time of writing.

Although ships have been taking on pilots for many centuries, it remains a moot point of law as to who has control of the ship and who is responsible for damage occurring to the ship. The standard entry by the Master in the deck log on taking a pilot on board reads 'Proceeding under Master's instructions and pilot's advice' is not accepted by members of the pilotage profession who will maintain that it is they who have the conduct of the vessel. Perhaps the clearest statement on the subject was made in the case of *The Tactician* (1907) 10 Asp MLC in which the court declared

'The cardinal principle to be bórne in mind in these cases ... is that the pilot is in sole charge of the ship, and that all directions as to speed, course, stopping and reversing and everything of that kind are for the pilot ... But side by side with that principle is the other principle that the pilot is entitled to the fullest assistance of a competent crew, a competent lookout, and a well-found ship.'

CHAPTER TWELVE

MARINAS & MOORINGS CONTRACTS

Unless his craft is of a size to be conveniently trailed behind a car and stored at home, a prime requirement for any yacht owner is a secure permanent mooring. A survey by the British Ports Federation in 1989 established the existence of over 150 000 permanent yacht moorings in British tidal waters, of which some 45 000 are in marinas (defined as pontoon berths with direct access to the shore).

The reasonable availability of a stock of moorings and marina berths is as much a necessity for a successful boat building trade as for the boat-owning public and the severe imbalance in supply and demand that caused prices to increase sharply in the late 1980s and early 1990s is thought by many to have done lasting damage to the industry. Apart from the substantial cost increases imposed on boat owners, a number of marina companies were also able to impose onerous contractual conditions on their customers who had the choice of simply accepting or trying to find alternative accommodation.

The establishment of berth holders' associations in many of the leading coastal marinas, and the sharp reduction in economic activity that followed the price increases, helped to even out the imbalances in the relative strength of the bargaining positions of the parties, so that the marina berth holder may now have a reasonable prospect of negotiating a fair price for his berthing as well as removing some of the unacceptable conditions referred to below which are still included in some contracts.

Yacht owners negotiating a marina berth need to carefully check the small print to ensure that they are not agreeing to onerous conditions and potentially crippling berthing charge reviews.

Marina's commission on sale of yacht

Although a decreasing number of marinas now impose a commission on the sale of yachts lying at their premises, the practice is still common enough to be of concern. The provision that 1% (or in some cases 2%) of the purchase price of a yacht sold privately or through a broker should be passed to the marina company is hard to justify. It is claimed that the responsibility of holding keys in safe keeping, verifying the identity of visitors wishing to look over a yacht, and of escorting visitors over the premises is sufficient to justify charging a commission. In practice the sale of a yacht takes place without the marina being put to any additional work or responsibility whatsoever, and if this provision is included in the standard contract, the sensible berth holder will ask for it to be deleted before entering into his annual agreement.

Where a marina company refuses to delete the provision from the contract, it should be noted that the British Boating Industry Code of Practice for the Sale of Second Hand Yachts provides that any such commission should be paid by the seller's broker (where one is involved) out of his commission, and should not be re-charged to the seller as an additional commission. It should also be noted that, according to the precise wording of the commission clause, it may be lawful for a seller to avoid paying any commission simply by removing his yacht from the marina at the relevant time that the sale takes place.

Access for external workers

A number of marinas still insist on all work on a berth holder's yacht being carried out by the marina's own staff, and either prohibiting access, or demanding a substantial access fee, from outside workers (disparagingly referred to as 'bagmen'). By way of justification it is claimed that the maintenance of a resident professional workforce on the site, and the payment of the necessary overhead expenses, requires the existence of a captive market, the loss of which would result in the workforce being disbanded and a poorer service being offered to berth holders. In fact experience at marinas where this provision is not imposed indicates that the level of service provided by external contractors is likely to be just as satisfactory, and in some cases very much less costly.

Work on the yacht within the marina

The conditions of berthing may also state no work may be done on the yacht by the owner or his crew other than minor running repairs or minor maintenance of a routine nature. This may be explained by the marina company as a necessity to prevent the sort of noise, clutter and disturbance that can be caused by an owner doing extensive work in an otherwise peaceful marina. However, since the standard conditions also have strict provisions about rubbish, noise, nuisance and annoyance sufficient to protect the interests of other berth holders, it does not appear necessary to limit an owner's right to work on his own boat provided he complies with those other rules.

Sub-letting a berth

The conditions will usually provide that the berth holder will not be entitled to the exclusive use of a particular berth, and all that is provided by the agreement is the provision of a general licence to berth that may involve several different berths in the course of the season. Additionally, unless the owner of the yacht has the prior consent of the marina operator, he may not lend or transfer the berth to another, the licence being personal, non-assignable, and relating only to a particular vessel. The clause will also usually provide that, having given notice in writing of an absence of more than 28 days, the berth holder may qualify for some part of any proceeds of re-letting his berth.

While it would be impractical for a marina company to guarantee a refund on an empty berth, it would be more equitable for the prospective berth holder to insist on a proportion of the letting income from the berth temporarily vacated by him to be credited to his account. If such a provision is agreed, it would be a sensible precaution to ask a neighbour to keep an eye on the berth since the records of the marina company may not always be entirely accurate.

Commercial activities

The conditions will usually state that no part of the marina or shore premises, or any vessel or vehicle on the premises, may be used by the owner for any commercial purposes. Such a provision is so widely drawn as to be virtually unenforceable, since it would not only exclude such obvious activities as a charter or sailing school business, but also any photography connected with advertising, the use of any sponsor's flags or logos, and even the use of vessels for entertaining business guests.

The purpose of such a contract term will usually be to require a higher level of berthing charges from those who are running their yachts on a commercial basis; the private owner who may make occasional use of his yacht in a business connection may wish this provision to be more clear in its definition of 'commercial purposes'.

Berth leasing

A growing practice in the late 1980s was for marina companies to offer extended berthing agreements, from as little as 3 years in some cases up to 40 years elsewhere. Expensively produced literature was produced to point out the rising demand for berths, the likelihood of ever-rising expenses, and the wisdom of providing for the future by paying a lump sum for up to 40 years' peace of mind.

While it is for each individual to do his own calculations, taking into account such imponderables as future economic cycles, likely supply and demand problems, planning restrictions, possible future boat taxes and so forth, there are matters that should be closely examined and discussed with the marina company.

Security of tenure

A fundamental concern to the berth holder should be the exact nature of the tenure. In many cases what is described as a lease is in fact no more than an extended licence. Whereas a lease actually transfers an interest in the land (in the case of a marina this would be the fundus directly below the pontoon and water area in question), a licence is, in law, no more than the landowner's consent for the licensee to be there. It is hard to see how, in a marina which is subject to tidal-induced movement, maintenance dredging, and occasional redesigning to increase the density of berthing, the precise area of fundus to be transferred can be sufficiently identified to create a valid lease. However, an exclusive licence can be as valuable as a lease, but the berth holder should know the exact nature of the interest he is enjoying, however it may be described in the sales literature.

Even if a valid lease is created, the lessee will want to know what will happen to his interest in the event of the landlord company going into liquidation. The days when marina ownership was regarded as a risk-free licence to print money have passed, and there are sufficient cases on record of marina companies either becoming insolvent, or surrendering leases back to the head landlord, to make the subsequent loss of a sub-lessor's interest a serious concern.

Service charges

The agreement for a long lease will normally provide for the payment of service charges on an annual basis to cover the manning and maintenance of the premises and pontoons. The service charge is normally fixed at a proportion of the full annual rate, but while the financial projections in the sales literature may assume a berthing rate (and thus a service charge) linked to the index of inflation, berthing rates can be very much more volatile. It might be possible for boat owners considering a long-term berth leasing arrangement to limit their service charge increase to the Retail Price Index.

Sub-letting of berths

Where an owner has taken the long lease of a berth, the agreement will normally provide for the sub-letting of the berth to third parties. Although in theory the marina company should not have the right to re-let vacant leased berths to short-term visitors, there will inevitably be occasions when they do so, and the owner should require all income from such short lets (less a commission for the marina company) to be credited to his service charge account. Here again it may be a wise precaution to ask a neighbour to keep an eye on the berth while the owner's yacht is away, in case the marina's record keeping should be unreliable.

Swinging moorings

For boat owners of more modest means, or those who wish to keep their yachts away from crowded marinas, an individual mooring on a tidal creek, estuary or alongside a river bank is the most likely alternative. Although there may be an infinite number of mooring sites around the country, the reality in modern times is that the chance of finding a free mooring in one of the more favoured boating areas is becoming remote. Particularly in areas such as the Crouch, the Hamble, Lymington and the more popular West Country rivers, it has been necessary to impose a rationing mechanism either by waiting list, a residents-only rule, or simply by pushing up the prices.

Where an individual wishes to take over a mooring patch and provide, lay and maintain his own ground tackle, it will normally be necessary for him to obtain a lease or licence from the owner of the fundus. There are around the country numerous areas where moorings have been laid for many years without the boat owner seeking the approval of the landlord, or offering any rent, or even being aware who the landlord may be. In such cases, particularly where the actual ground tackle has remained in precisely the same position over the years, it may be possible for the boat owner to have established a possessory title. In effect this means that if he has been on the site for 12 years without dispute he can defend an action to remove him, after 20 years he may claim ownership of the site against a private landlord and after 60 years he may claim ownership even against the Crown. In practice, the modest rents usually asked by landlords of the fundus have made it unrealistic for mooring owners to risk large sums to assert their legal rights, once the landlord has woken up to the situation and started to demand a rent. As a result, the payment of a licence fee or rent, however modest, effectively destroys the possessory title of the mooring owner since the payments act as an acknowledgement of the landlord's title.

Where the landlord's title is acknowledged, the main question at issue will be the value to be put on the mooring. In arriving at a value, the same principles apply as to a lease of land, namely what a willing tenant is prepared to pay to a willing landlord, and the best guide is the existence of comparable rents. In an era of high demand for mooring areas by established boat owners and increasing numbers of newcomers to the sport, coupled with artificial limits on the supply of moorings being imposed by planning

An open-sea mooring may be cheaper but is it insurable?

authorities and harbour boards, normally at the behest of conservation bodies or local residents who do not wish to see the area
crowded with incomers, there is likely to be considerable upward
pressure on mooring rents as landlords profit from the situation.
We are fortunate in this country in that the major public landlords
such as the Crown Estate Commissioners, and the Duchies of
Lancaster and Cornwall recognise the importance of keeping rents
to a reasonable level to avoid causing hardship to boat owners on a
low income, although even these bodies have on occasion been
criticised for jumping on the bandwagon in times of high demand.

However, since mooring rents are always a matter for negotiation,
the mooring owner's best response to a demand for an unreasonably
high rent is to create an association of owners with a similar interest
in the area to negotiate on its members' behalf, and ideally to take a
management lease of the entire area to deal with the administration
of all the moorings on a co-operative basis.

Mooring area leases are customarily taken by boat clubs, harbour
authorities and by local authorities wishing to provide a service for

their local rate payers. In most cases the landlords will be one of the major public bodies referred to above, and here again the same valuation principles apply. In fact the additional bargaining power of the larger tenants does not appear necessarily to work in their favour. In 1990 the Lymington Harbour Commissioners, renewing an old mooring lease, were required to acknowledge an increase in ground rent value from £3000 pa to over £100 000 pa for the private yacht moorings provided by them on fundus owned by the Crown. It would have been possible for the Commissioners to refuse to renew the lease on such terms, and to have left the Crown to deal direct with the individual boat owners (as is the case at Poole where the Harbour Commissioners successfully manage the entire harbour, but only lease a core area), but the Commissioners appeared to find this an unacceptable alternative.

Rating of moorings

Local authority policy on the rating of moorings varies from one area to another, according to the type of mooring concerned, and according to the use to which it is put. There are four essential ingredients for occupation to be rateable, the absence of any one of which will entitle the occupier to refuse a rates demand.

1　There must be actual occupation or possession

2　The occupation must be exclusive for the particular purposes of the possessor

3　Possession must be of some value or benefit to the possessor

4　Possession must not be for too transient a period

Before rates can be levied on the occupation of land, it must be established that the land in question lies within the local authority rating area. In most cases the boundary stops at the low water mark, although in certain specific areas (including Brighton, Torquay, Lowestoft and Southwold), areas below the low water mark have been added by private Act of Parliament. Similarly, where both banks of a tidal creek or river lie within the area of a local authority the entire water area will come under its jurisdiction unless it is so wide that, in the test applied in ancient case law, a man cannot see what is being done on the far bank.

In the passage through Parliament of the 1984 Rates Act, boating interests led by the Royal Yachting Association lobbied successfully for the codification and amendment of the law affecting the rating of moorings. The result is that moorings are exempt from rates provided they are:

- Used or intended to be used by a boat or ship
- Equipped only with a buoy attached to an anchor, weight, or other device resting on, or in the bed of the sea, river or other water, and designed to be raised from the bed from time to time

This in effect means that all 'swinging' moorings of the conventional type are exempt, whether secured by a single block, anchor or weight, or attached to a ground chain, or to a series of anchors, provided they are designed to be raised for renewal or inspection from time to time. Also exempt are fore-and-aft moorings of the same general design as swinging moorings, where the yacht has a buoy at either end. Not exempt, clearly, are driven pile moorings and screw pile moorings, and other permanently fixed and bank-side structures.

Prior to the 1984 Rates Act the local authority Valuation Officer was required to assess and collect rates from moorings individually; the Act provided that moorings may now be assessed collectively and rates collected from the authority controlling and receiving the fees for moorings. This only applies to fixed moorings, but in effect transfers to the club, harbour authority or marina owner the responsibility for collecting a contribution to the local assessment from each of the mooring holders. If an individual mooring holder suspects he is being charged for more than his fair share, he may apply to have his mooring separately assessed.

CHAPTER THIRTEEN

GOING FOREIGN

A boat owner intending to cruise overseas must take care to comply with all the legal formalities involved both within the UK and in the countries he intends to visit.

Documentation

Firstly he should ensure that the ship's papers are in order; these will include a registration certificate with the correct particulars and which will remain valid for the duration of the voyage, any relevant charter contract, and his insurance policy and certificate. For VAT paid craft, the original VAT invoice should be carried, or alternatively a Single Administration Document issued by HM Customs and Excise to certify either that VAT has been paid, or that the craft was over eight years old *and* was within the territory of the European Community on 31 December 1992 (when the single fiscal area came into being). Where a yacht is lent, the skipper should have a letter of authority from the owner whose name appears on the registration certificate. The letter should specify the name and address of the borrower, and state that the vessel is being used by him with the consent of the owner for the period specified and within the cruising range, or the voyage, specified.

Where a yacht is being used under a charter agreement, it is essential that the charter contract as well as the registration certificate is aboard.

A Radio-Telephone Ship Licence is required for every vessel with R/T equipment on board, available from the Radio

Communications Agency at the Department of Trade and Industry (see Appendix 6 for address). It is also necessary for the intended operator to have the necessary operator's licence according to the class of radio carried on board. In the case of a VHF set, examination and licence arrangements are made through the RYA.

The skipper and crew will also need passports and any necessary visas. In most cases a visa can be obtained at the port of entry, but in some states this is not possible and unless it has been acquired in advance, entry into the state may be prohibited.

Flags

Under international law all ships should wear their national colours when in foreign territorial waters; in practice the convention is for British yachts to wear their colours (either the Red Ensign or a privileged ensign) at all times when manned except when in harbour between sunset and sunrise. The international code flag Q (my vessel is healthy and I request free pratique) should also be carried and worn when clearing in foreign ports or back in the UK after going foreign. This is not required for voyages between EC states.

Courtesy flags for each of the states to be visited (whether within the EC or not) should also be carried.

Insurance

Although insurance in most foreign states (or the UK) is not compulsory, it makes sense to be comprehensively insured for the area likely to be covered in the cruise. This may need to be extended if it is intended to use continental inland canals and rivers. Reciprocal medical expense arrangements can be made with all EC states by obtaining and completing the appropriate Certificates of Entitlement from the owner's local Benefits Agency office prior to departure.

It should be noted that third party insurance is compulsory for all pleasure craft in Italy, and if it is intended to visit Italian waters the insurance policy and an Italian translation of the insurance certificate (available from all British insurance companies) must be carried aboard. Failure to do so may result in the boat being impounded and the crew being required to stay ashore until the necessary documentation is obtained.

Notice of departure

Owners of yachts cruising outside the EC should obtain and complete Customs Form C1331; Notice of Intended Departure and Report of Arrival Declaration, obtainable free of charge from most Customs offices, harbour authorities, marinas and yacht clubs. The top part of the form must be completed with details of the yacht and crew and posted to the Customs (either by mail or in a Customs letter box) prior to departure.

So far as cruises to other EC states are concerned, on 1 January 1993 the European Community became a 'Single Market' which in the words of Article 8A of the Treaty of Rome is 'an area without internal frontiers in which the free movement of goods, persons, services and capital is ensured'. In effect this means that there are no reporting out or reporting in requirements for British yachts cruising to other EC countries provided that there are no non-EC residents aboard, and no prohibited or restricted goods such as firearms, animals, drugs or other goods in excess of the normal allowance.

Foreign arrival

On arrival at an overseas port the national colours and local courtesy flag must be flown, as well as the Q-flag in the case of a non-EC state. There may also be local formalities to be completed, which vary from country to country and port to port. For most European states details of such formalities are contained in the RYA publication, *Planning a Foreign Cruise*. For those going further overseas, membership of the Cruising Association gives access to their comprehensive chartroom and library; detailed planning of cruises well in advance will pay dividends in ensuring that the correct documents and information required by officials in the host country are immediately available. In most cases, it will be useful to have duplicate copies of the full details of the yacht, as well as a full crew list with surname, forename, date and place of birth, function on board, passport number and nationality. If all this information is available on a single sheet, this can greatly reduce the time spent in completing entry formalities in each new country visited.

Returning to the UK

For craft returning from outside the EC (and this includes those cruising *directly* from Gibraltar, the Channel Islands, the Isle of

Man and the Spanish Canaries), strict requirements are in force from the 12-mile limit. Form C1331 must be completed and deposited with the Customs office or in a Customs post box, and the local Customs office must be contacted by phone with the following details:

- Name of the vessel
- Last port of call
- Location of mooring or marina berth
- Whether the vessel is tax-paid in any EC state
- Nationality and number of all crew members
- Whether any prohibited or restricted goods are on board, including animals, firearms, controlled drugs, or excess stores
- Whether there has been any death or notifiable disease on board

Rabies

Much publicity has been given in recent years to the spread of rabies on mainland Europe, and to the very strict UK quarantine regulations for animals. At present the United Kingdom is free of rabies, but the potential threat arising from irresponsible owners taking their pets overseas in caravans or boats, and then attempting to bring them back into the country, has always caused any yacht with animals aboard to be treated with suspicion. Indeed in Ramsgate Harbour local byelaws prohibit the keeping of any domestic animals on boats.

For foreign vessels coming into UK waters, the Rabies Act provides that any animals on board must be securely confined in a totally enclosed part of the vessel, prevented from making contact with any other animal, and in no circumstances being permitted to land.

Driving licences

Although there is no requirement in any waters in the UK, whether inland or tidal, for private pleasure craft owners to have a certificate of competence, there are a number of such requirements overseas, including certain EC states. From 1993 the Dutch authorities have required the drivers of fast (over 20 kph) or large (over 15 metres) powered craft on their estuarial or inland waters to be licensed to take a written examination for a driver's licence. For British boat owners exemption is given for those qualified to the Royal Yachting Association Coastal Yachtmaster level.

From 1994 the French authorities have required the drivers of all craft on their inland rivers and canals to be licensed; for craft under 15 metres in length and capable of less than 20 kph again there is an exemption for British owners who are in possession of a Helmsman's Overseas Certificate of Competence. This document is issued by the RYA to applicants who have either passed a boat-handling test at a Recognised Teaching Establishment, or who have been certified as competent by the Principal of such an establishment or a flag officer of any club affiliated to the RYA.

There are a number of bodies, official and semi-official, within the European Community who would wish to see the introduction of compulsory driving licences in all EC states. As small, fast, recreational craft grow in numbers, and rivers and coastal waters become even more crowded, some feel that it is only a matter of time before compulsory driving licences for these craft become the norm rather than the exemption in Europe.

CHAPTER FOURTEEN

POLLUTION

It is only in recent years that any form of pollution controls have been applied to yachtsmen generally. Although most canals and navigable rivers have had restrictions on the use of marine toilets, general pollution controls have been restricted to large passenger and freight ships, and oil tankers.

In 1988 the International Convention for the Prevention of Pollution from Ships (MARPOL) came into effect, Annex V of which comprises the Garbage Control Regulations which have now been adopted by the British Government. In the Regulations 'Garbage' is defined as 'all victual, domestic and operational waste, excluding fresh fish and parts thereof'. The controls established by Annex V, which extend to cover pleasure yachts, are strict, and vary accordingly to the type of garbage and the area in which the vessel is operating.

The Convention bans absolutely the dumping of all plastics, including synthetic ropes, nets and garbage bags, in any tidal waters in the world. For non-plastic lining and packaging material which can float, the regulations provide that it may not be dropped overboard within 25 miles of land, or anywhere within the particularly vulnerable 'special areas' which include the North Sea. Food wastes and other garbage, including paper products, rags, glass, metal, bottles, crockery etc may not be dumped within 12 miles of land (or anywhere within a 'special area') while ground-up food wastes, and all other garbage broken down to 25 millimetre segments, may only be dropped more than 3 miles from land (or 25 miles from land in special areas).

A further development to the existing MARPOL convention is the requirement for all craft (including pleasure craft with accommodation for ten or more people) to fit and use holding tanks for their domestic sewage, and not to discharge it into the sea within 12 miles of the nearest land. Each party to the Convention will be required to provide adequate pump-out facilities for holding tanks at all ports. Also, in 1990, the Ministerial Conference on the North Sea agreed to introduce immediate measures to control the discharge of sewage into the coastal zones of the North Sea, from all ships with a complement of 50 or more, on voyages between North Sea ports, irrespective of the coming into effect of the MARPOL Convention on sewage discharges.

Antifouling paints

Before the mid-1980s there had been no controls on the specification and content of marine antifoulings. Traditionally most antifoulings had been copper-based, with some users adding a lacing of arsenic or mercury for extra effect. The adoption of tributyl-tin in the late 1970s produced an antifouling that gave a far better performance, and over a period of time tin became the standard killing agent in most antifouling paints. By 1985 the Ministry of Agriculture, Fisheries and Food had started to receive complaints from oyster farmers that, on oyster beds situated near popular mooring areas, oysters were suffering from poor growth and from thickening and delaminating shells. The earliest evidence was limited to imported Japanese Oyster stocks, this being a species introduced to give a higher growth rate, while the native oyster (*Ostrea edulis*) appeared unaffected by tin in the water.

Early Government proposals to ban TBT were vigorously opposed by boat owners and paintmakers alike, since there was no evidence that any natural shellfish in UK waters were being adversely affected. However, within 12 months there had been sufficient advances in atomic spectrography analysis to show that even the slightest traces (measured in one part of TBT per billion parts of water) were capable of doing damage to other, non-commercial, species of shellfish, and by common consent tin-based antifoulings were withdrawn from sale.

The industry then reverted to the traditional copper-based antifoulings, but in a more efficient form. Regulations introduced under the Control of Pollution Act 1974 now required all new antifouling paints to be submitted to the Department of the Environment for approval before being allowed on to the market.

Engine noise

Although there is no nationally imposed standard for the control of engine noise, most inland waterways and harbour areas have byelaws in place to require that all engines are 'effectively silenced'. This local legislation, coupled with improved technology, has resulted in recent years in greatly reduced noise levels, particularly for outboard engines and personal watercraft. The reduction of engine noise has led to research being directed to hull-generated noise, which is a particular cause of complaint on some of the larger inland lakes. On Windermere, where pressure has existed for a great many years for the imposition of a speed limit, the level of complaints about hull noise in choppy conditions is as great as that over engine noise.

Exhaust emissions

Despite great strides being made in the reduction of emissions from road vehicles, at the time of writing comparatively little attention has been paid to boat exhausts. In 1989 a proposal for joint Swiss, Austrian and German regulations was put forward for controls on Lake Constance. Draft regulations were later submitted to the European Commission for approval, which, if eventually given, will make it only a matter of time before an Emission Directive is issued to cover all waters within the jurisdiction of EC states.

Sewage treatment

Although the prospect of exhaust emission and noise controls, and the present garbage and antifouling regulations operate to restrict the activities of boat owners, the 'green revolution' has brought direct benefits in the cleaning up of sailing waters suffering from sewage pollution.

In 1989 the Water Act came into effect, giving responsibility for setting water quality standards, and monitoring progress, to the National Rivers Authority. The water supply companies, privatised in 1990, were given targets for the reduction and eventual ending of raw sewage being discharged into the sea except from very small coastal communities in non-sensitive areas.

Although the main concerns of the NRA are directed towards bathing beaches, and this is also the focus of the European Commission 'Blue Flag' beach standards Scheme, the interest generated by this activity has led to better understanding of the effects of sewage pollution on water users. Whereas a bad cold or influenza symptoms after a swim would previously have been attributed to a chill, there is now incontestable proof that the bacteria and viruses contained in raw sewage cause these complaints, as well as evidence that hepatitis, meningitis and salmonella may be contracted. The research carried out for the cleaning up of bathing beaches has been of value to windsurfers, dinghy sailors and coastal cruisers.

The increasing pressure for a prohibition on all discharges of significant amounts of sewage will without a doubt make our near-inshore waters very much more pleasant to sail in. However serious worries still exist that removal of the bacteria necessary to comply with the EC Bathing Water Directive will still permit the existence of other bacteria and viruses likely to cause ear, nose and throat infections, gastro intestinal infections, respiratory disorders and viral infections.

CHAPTER FIFTEEN

TRAILING

The law relating to the safe trailing of boats on the public highway has become very much more detailed with the issue of European Directives on road safety. This chapter states the law in October 1993 and although the general principles stated will remain, some of the details about marking of projections, lighting, and speed limits may vary from time to time. The rules about overall dimensions, projections etc are unlikely to be subject to the same change.

Modern trailers make light work of launching!

General duty to make loads and projections safe

All vehicles and trailers, and their parts and accessories, must at all times be kept in such condition that no possible danger is caused to any person. The same principle applies to the weight, distribution and adjustment of any load carried on a vehicle or trailer. Even if an overhanging mast or protruding outboard motor does not infringe any of the detailed size limitations set out below, carrying or towing it will nonetheless contravene the law if by doing so a possible danger is caused to other road users. Fines can be imposed if this principle or any of the other regulations are breached. Anyone injured could make a civil claim against the person responsible. Trailers and their loads should therefore be carefully maintained, secured and protected. Loads on roof-racks should be secure and where necessary marked, protected and lit.

Insurance

The towing vehicle and the boat/trailer combination should be separately insured. Vehicle insurers should be told if it is to be used for towing. Liability for damage caused by the boat/trailer combination when:

●   attached to the towing vehicle; or
●   after it has become accidentally detached from it

should be covered under the third party liability section of the vehicle policy. Damage caused *to* the boat/trailer would have to be claimed under the boat policy.

When the boat/trailer has been deliberately detached from the towing vehicle, any liability for damage caused *by* it must be claimed under the boat policy.

Length restrictions

The trailer itself
A trailer towed by an ordinary car must not be longer than 7 metres (excluding the hitching device) nor wider than 2.3 metres. If towing with a goods vehicle weighing more than 3500 kg and the trailer has at least 4 wheels then the trailer may be up to 12 metres long.

The trailer and towing vehicle combination
The maximum permitted overall length of the trailer and tow vehi-

cle combination is 18 metres (*excluding* projecting parts of the load). However if the trailer is constructed and normally used for carrying an 'indivisible load of exceptional length' such as a boat, then:

- the overall length of the towing vehicle must not exceed 9.2 metres and
- the overall length of the combination of vehicles must not exceed 25.9 metres *including* any projection of the load; if it does, the police must be notified in advance, and an assistant carried

Roof-rack loads

The maximum permitted length of a load carried on a single vehicle is 18.3 metres, which is much longer than could safely be carried on either a passenger car or small commercial vehicle. Restrictions on roof-rack loads will therefore be governed by the rules relating to projections, detailed below.

Width restrictions

It is important to distinguish between

- the permitted width of the trailer itself
- the extent to which a load may project on either side of the trailer
- the overall width of the trailer and the load carried on it

Trailers towed by ordinary cars should not be wider than 2.3 metres. If the towing vehicle weighs more than 3500 kg, this width can be up to 2.5 metres.

No load should project more than 305 millimetres sideways from the trailer, nor may the total width of the trailer and any sideways projection exceed 2.9 metres.

The effect of these rules is that boats up to 2.9 metres wide may be carried on standard trailers. If a boat wider than 2.9 metres is to be towed, the police should be notified in advance. If the boat width exceeds 3.5 metres then the police must be notified in advance and an assistant carried. The maximum permitted width of a load is 4.3 metres.

Height restrictions

There is no legal maximum height for a boat trailer and its load, or for a load carried on a motor vehicle. However, the general rule requiring that loads be safely attached and distributed should be borne in mind. The trailer manufacturing industry suggest a maximum height of 3 metres, or 1.7 times the wheel track of the trailer, to be good practice. Equipment should always be stored so as to keep the centre of gravity of the load as low as possible.

Front and rear overhangs

Subject to certain conditions a load may extend beyond the front or rear of, or be wider than, a vehicle carrying it. The regulations use the terms 'forward and rearward projection' and define these as being those parts of the load which extend beyond the foremost and rearmost points of the vehicle on which the load rests.

Projections may need to be marked, protected and lit.

Marking: forward projections
If more than 2 metres, an assistant must be carried and end and side marker boards fitted. If more than 3.05 metres, the police must be notified in advance. If more than 4.5 metres, extra side marker boards must be fitted.

Marking: rearward projections
If the rear projection of the load exceeds 1 metre, it must be marked so as to be clearly visible, both to the rear and on both sides (eg by using a bright red or orange plastic bag or rag).

A rearward projection extending between 2 metres and 3.05 metres must be fitted with an end marker board. If it extends beyond 3.05 metres a rear marker board and two side marker boards are needed, the police must be told in advance and an assistant must be carried. Extra side marker boards are needed if the rearward projection exceeds 5 metres.

End marker boards should be triangular, with two sides of equal length. The triangle base and height must both be not less than 610 millimetres and the board should be marked with alternate red and white stripes. Side marker boards should consist of similarly marked right angle triangular boards not less than 610 millimetres in height and 1520 millimetres in length.

Protection
All projections should be protected so as not to be capable of causing any danger. It is particularly important to protect the exposed blades of an outboard motor mounted on a boat's transom; there have been a number of prosecutions for failure to do so.

Weights of motor vehicles and trailers

The Regulations use the following weight definitions:

Axle weight The sum of weights transmitted to the road surface by that axle.

Gross weight   (a) In relation to the motor vehicle, the sum of the weight transmitted to the road surface by all the wheels of the vehicle.
(b) In relation to a trailer, the sum of all the weights transmitted to the road and of any weight of the trailer imposed on the drawing vehicle.

Maximum gross weight (a) In the case of a trailer equipped with a rating plate, the maximum gross weight shown on the plate.
(b) In any other case, the weight which the trailer is designed or adapted not to exceed when travelling by road.

Kerbside weight (a) In the case of a motor vehicle, its weight when it carries no person and no load other than loose tools and equipment with which it is normally equipped and a full supply of fuel in its tank.

Make sure you give your yacht a good lashing before you travel. This Leisure 17 will need at least a nose lashing, and two webbing cross straps (ideally tightened with racket buckles) to keep it secure.

(b) In the case of a trailer, its weight when carrying no person and is otherwise unladen.

Laden weight/Gross weight, in relation to a trailer, both mean the unladen (or kerbside) weight of the trailer plus any load it is carrying. The relevant weights can be checked using a local weighbridge.

There are no prescribed minimum power/weight ratios for passenger car and trailer combinations. The weight of a goods vehicle must not exceed 1000 kg for each 4.4 kW of engine power. Boat owners should always bear in mind the overall requirement for the vehicle/trailer/load combination to be roadworthy.

Weight marking

Unbraked trailers are required to be marked, in a conspicuous place on the nearside, with the maximum gross weight. Heavy goods vehicle trailers exceeding 1020 kg unladen weight must carry a plate showing the details specified in Schedule 8 to the Construction and Use Regulations.

Brakes

All trailers must be fitted with brakes if either:

- the sum of the trailer's design axle weights exceeds 750 kg; or
- its laden weight exceeds its maximum gross weight; or
- the laden weight of the trailer exceeds half the towing vehicle's kerbside weight.

All trailers required to be fitted with brakes must also be equipped with a parking brake.

Trailers first used before 1 April 1983 may be fitted with overrun or 'inertia' brakes which apply automatically if the trailer overruns. Such brakes must be efficient but no specific performance level is set.

Trailers first used from 1 April 1983 may also be fitted with overrun brakes but couplings must be damped and matched with the brake linkage. Brake design should have undergone a type approval test and braking efficiency must be at least 45%. The parking brake must be capable of holding the laden trailer on an 18% gradient. Trailers should also be fitted with an emergency device which will stop the trailer automatically if it becomes uncoupled. This does not apply to a single-axle trailer up to 1500 kg maximum gross weight if fitted with a chain or cable which will prevent the coupling head from touching the ground if it becomes uncoupled.

Heavier trailers must have brakes, and trailers in excess of 3500 kg total laden weight must have fully powered brakes operated by the braking system of the towing vehicle.

Tyres

It is illegal to mix cross ply and radial tyres on the same axle of a trailer. It is essential that tyres are suitable for the use to which they are being put, have a sufficient depth of tread and be free from any defect which might in any way cause damage either to the road surface, persons in the towing vehicle, or other persons using the road. Tyres must be correctly inflated; advice on correct inflation pressure should be obtained from the trailer manufacturer or tyre supplier. The tyres of trailers first used after April 1987 must be designed and maintained to support the trailer's maximum axle weight at its maximum permitted speed of 60 mph.

Minimum tyre tread depth
With effect from 1 January 1992, the minimum legal tread depth for car and trailer tyres is 1.6 millimetres. The tyre standards provide that 'the grooves of the tread pattern shall be of a depth of at least 1.6 millimetres throughout a continuous band comprising the central three quarter of the breadth of tread and round the entire circumference of the tyre'.

The standard applies to:

- *cars* meaning passenger vehicles which can carry up to 8 seated passengers in addition to the driver
- *light goods vehicles* (such as light vans) which have a maximum gross weight of up to 3500 kg
- *light trailers* which have a maximum gross weight of up to 3500 kg

The maximum penalty for driving a vehicle with less than the legal minimum of tread depth is a fine of £1000.

Suspension, bearings, mudguards and registration plate

For those who trail long distances, it may be an advantage to have larger wheels than the manufacturer's normal specification. Trailers bought from manufacturers can be expected to comply with the regulations. If building a trailer or renovating an old one, bear in mind that it must be fitted with suspension and mudguards. Efficient suspension is important because the road impact on a small wheel is large and it is more likely to collapse than a car wheel. For those who are proposing the home building of a trailer, careful study of the component manufacturer's recommendations is advisable.

If a road trailer is immersed while launching a boat, there is considerable risk of subsequent corrosion both to bearing surfaces and those parts of the trailer framework which may retain water. Corrosion is likely to be particularly severe if there is immersion in salt water; this should be avoided whenever possible. Hosing down well after immersion is essential.

The trailer registration number plate must be identical in shape, colour and characteristics to the plate on the towing vehicle. It must be illuminated at night.

Lighting

The 1989 Lighting Regulations introduced a number of changes affecting the lighting of boat trailers. The table opposite summarises these rules.

Wide loads, or loads which overhang the carrying vehicle or trailer, may need to be fitted with extra lights and reflectors.

The lighting of wide trailers and wide trailer loads
Boat trailers generally need not carry white front position lamps. However:

- a trailer which projects sideways more than 400 millimetres beyond the illuminated area of the towing vehicle's front position lamp on that side must fit a forward facing white lamp
- a trailer whose load projects in a similar way must have a forward facing white lamp fitted to either the trailer or the load

Regulation 21 specifies in detail how these lamps should be fitted.

The lighting of overhanging loads
Additional lamps and reflectors must be fitted to loads which project (forward or rearward) more than 1 metre beyond the carrying vehicle or the trailer.

A load projecting rearwards more than 1 metre (whether on a motor vehicle or trailer) must be lit by an additional rear lamp and a red retro-reflector fitted not more than 1 metre from the rear of the load. In practice, the need for such a lamp is usually avoided when carrying an overhanging boat on a trailer by either fitting an extension to the trailer, so that the rear lighting board is positioned vertically below the rearmost part of the load, or by fitting the lighting board to the transom of the boat. If either of these methods

Summary of lighting requirements for boat trailers

Type of trailer	Source in 1989 Regs of detailed information	Lights required
All trailers, irrespective of age or size	Schedule 10 Part I	2 rear red position lamps
	Schedule 12 Part I	2 rear red stop lamps
	Schedule 15	Rear white registration plate lamp(s)
	Schedule 7 Part I	2 rear red retro-reflectors (maximum of 400 mm from the side of the trailer)
Trailers manufactured after 1 September 1965	Schedule 7 Part I	2 rear amber direction indicators
Trailers manufactured after 1 April 1980	Schedule 11 Part I	1 rear red fog lamp
Trailers manufactured after 1 October 1990	Schedule 21 Part I	2 non-triangular white forward facing retro-reflectors
Trailers manufactured after 1 October 1990 *and* wider than 2.1 m Note: trailer, not load, width	Schedule 13 Part I	2 forward facing white end-outline marker lamps 2 rearward facing red end-outline marker lamps (White and red lamps on one side of a trailer may be combined into a single lamp with a single light source)
Trailers longer than 5 m (excluding hitching device and load overhang)	Schedule 17 Part I	At least 2 (and more as required by length) amber side facing retro-reflectors on each side of trailer (Reflectors within 1m of rear may be red)
Trailers whose gross maximum weight exceeds 3500 kg (unless manufactured before 1 August 1982 with an unladen weight of less than 1020 kg)	Schedule 19 Part I	Rear marking board composed of red fluorescent and yellow retro-reflecting stripes Note: this requirement does not apply to a trailer carrying two or more boats

of fitting is adopted, care should be taken that a boat mast does not overhang the aft end of the boat by more than 1 metre.

A lighting board should not be positioned more than 1.5 metres from the ground (or 2.1 metres 'if the structure of the vehicle makes this impracticable'). Trailers made before 1 October 1985 are permitted to have their rear lamps up to 2.1 metres above the ground.

A load which is carried on a motor vehicle and which projects forward more than 1 metre from the front of the vehicle must be lit by an additional front facing white lamp and white retro-reflector fitted not more than 1 metre from the front end of the load.

Using a boat trailer on the road

Driving licence
A vehicle towing a trailer should not be driven by the holder of a provisional licence.

Speeds
The speed limit for towing a trailer behind a passenger car is 50 mph, or 60 mph on motorways and dual carriageways.

Towing on motorways and dual carriageways
Towing is not permitted in the outside lane of a three or four lane carriageway or motorway, or at any place where all three lanes are open for use by traffic proceeding in the same direction, except when passing another vehicle of such exceptional width that it can only be passed by entering such a lane.

On a two-lane carriageway or motorway, both lanes may be used.

Detached trailers
A trailer detached from the towing vehicle and left to stand on a road must have at least one wheel prevented from revolving, either by means of a brake, chain, chock or other efficient device. Failure to do so is an offence.

A detached trailer left to stand on the road between sunset and sunrise must be lit. This means that every

- rear position lamp
- rear registration plate lamp
- side marker lamp
- end out-line marker lamp

must be kept lit and unobscured. Boat trailers need not normally be fitted with front position lamps when attached to the towing vehicle, but these lamps must be fitted and lit before the trailer is left detached on a road at night.

AGREEMENT FOR THE SALE OF A SECOND-HAND YACHT

An agreement prepared by the Royal Yachting Association for the sale of a second-hand yacht between persons not normally engaged in the business of selling yachts.

AN AGREEMENT made the   day of   19

BETWEEN :

1. 'The Vendor' :
   of

2. 'The Purchaser' :
   of

The terms 'Vendor' and 'Purchaser' include their respective successors in title and the Vendor and Purchaser shall hereinafter be collectively referred to as 'the Parties'.

'The Purchase Price' :   sterling

'The Deposit'   : 10% of the Purchase Price

In respect of the sale of a [REGISTERED/UNREGISTERED] PLEASURE CRAFT

Name :
Description :
Official No. :
Port of Registry where applicable :
Now lying at :

Including all equipment, machinery and gear on board ('the Yacht') and any specific inventory attached hereto initialled by the Parties and forming part of this Agreement.

Agreement for sale

1. The Vendor hereby agrees to sell and the Purchaser agrees to purchase the Yacht free from any encumbrances (subject to the conditions and terms of this agreement), together with all her outfit gear and equipment as set out in a schedule hereto but not including stores or the Vendor's personal effects, for the Purchase Price.

Payment
of deposit

2.   On the signing of this agreement the Deposit is to be paid to the Vendor and the balance of the Purchase Price together with any Value Added Tax shall be payable in accordance with Clause 6.

Value
Added Tax

3.1   The Vendor [is/is not] a registered person for the purpose of the regulations relating to Value Added Tax and the Purchase Price [is/is not] exclusive of Value Added Tax.

Import
dues and
local taxes
(craft lying
overseas)

3.2   The Vendor warrants that the craft has been properly [temporarily/permanently] imported into [   ] and that all appropriate local taxes and dues have been paid and that the proposed sale is in accordance with all relevant local laws and regulations.

Inspection
survey

4.   The Purchaser may, at a venue to be agreed and at his own cost, haul out or place ashore and/or open up the Yacht and her machinery for the purposes of inspection and/or survey which, including any written report, shall be completed within [   ] days of the signing of this agreement. If any inspection requires more than superficial non-destructive dismantling the consent of the Vendor must be obtained before such work commences.

Notice
of defects

5.1   Within fourteen days after completion of such inspection and/or survey if any material defect(s) in the Yacht or her machinery other than disclosed to the Purchaser in writing prior to the signing of this agreement or any material deficiencies in her inventory, if any, shall have been found the Purchaser may either :

5.1.1   give notice to the Vendor of his rejection of the Yacht provided that the notice shall specify any material defect(s) or deficiencies; or

5.1.2   give notice to the Vendor specifying any material defect(s) or deficiencies and requiring the Vendor forthwith either to make good the same or make a sufficient reduction in the Purchase Price to enable the Purchaser to make good the same. All agreed items of work to be completed without undue delay in all circumstances and to be carried out so as to satisfy the expressly specified requirements of the Purchaser's surveyor in respect only of material defects mentioned in his report and specified in the notice to the Vendor.

5.2   If the Purchaser shall have served a notice of rejection under Clause 5.1.1, then this agreement shall be deemed to be rescinded forthwith and the Vendor shall refund to the purchaser the Deposit in accordance with Clause 8.

5.3 If the Purchaser shall have served a notice under Clause 5.1.2 requiring the Vendor to make good material defects or deficiencies or to make a reduction in the Purchase Price, and the Vendor shall not have agreed within twenty one days after the service of the notice to make good such defects or the Parties have not agreed in the twenty one days after the service of notice upon the reduction in the Purchase Price, then this agreement shall be deemed to have been rescinded on the twenty second day after the service of notice and the Vendor shall refund to the Purchaser the Deposit in accordance with Clause 8.

In the case of any deficiencies in the Yacht's inventory (if any) remaining or arising within seven days of acceptance in accordance with Clause 6 the deficiencies shall be made good or a reduction in the Purchase Price shall be agreed, failing which this agreement shall be rescinded at the option of the Purchaser only.

Acceptance of Yacht

6.1 The Yacht shall be deemed to have been accepted by the Purchaser and the balance of the Purchase Price and any Value Added Tax thereon shall become due and payable in accordance with Clause 7 upon the happening of any of the following events :

6.2 The expiry of fourteen days from the date of this agreement or such extended period as may be agreed between the Parties provided that no inspection or survey has been commenced;

6.3 The expiry of fifteen days from the completion of the survey, provided that the Purchaser has not served notice under Clause 5.1;

6.4 Notification in writing by the Vendor to the Purchaser of completion of the remedial works specified in a notice given by the Purchaser under Clause 5.1.2.

Completion of Sale

7.1 Upon acceptance of the Yacht by the Purchaser, the Deposit shall be treated as part payment of the Purchase Price. Within seven days of acceptance the Purchaser shall pay the balance of the Purchase Price and any Value Added Tax thereon and the Vendor shall :

In the case of a registered yacht

Registered
Yacht

7.1.1 provide the Purchaser with the Certificate of Registry, correct and updated, together with any other documents appertaining to the Yacht and shall execute a Bill of Sale, in the prescribed form, in favour of the Purchaser or his nominee, showing the Yacht to be free from encumbrances and completed so as to ensure transfer on the Register; OR

7.1.2 *In the case of an unregistered yacht* (including a yacht registered on the SSR)

Unregistered
or SSR
Registered
Yacht

(a) Provide the Purchaser with a Bill of Sale in favour of the Purchaser or his nominee, together with any other documents appertaining to the Yacht;

(b) Deliver to the Purchaser any necessary delivery order or other authority enabling the Purchaser to take immediate possession of the Yacht.

7.2 Where payment is made by cheque, draft, letter of credit or other instrument, the terms of this agreement shall not be deemed to have been fulfilled until such payment is cleared into the payee's account.

Vendor's
right to
assign title

7.3 By delivery of the documents specified in either case the Vendor shall be deemed to have covenanted AND HEREBY COVENANTS that he has the right to transfer property in the Yacht and that the same is free from all encumbrances, debts, liens and the like except such encumbrances and liabilities for duties, taxes, debts, liens and the like as are the responsibility of the Purchaser under Clauses 4 and 8.

Free
access after
completion

7.4 On completion, the Vendor shall ensure that the Yacht is available for collection by the Purchaser and that free access by the Purchaser together with all necessary haulage equipment is permitted at no additional cost to the Purchaser.

Rescission
of
agreement

8.1 In the event of rescission of this agreement by the Purchaser he shall, at his own expense, reinstate the Yacht to the condition and position in which he found her, and shall pay all boatyard and surveyor's charges for this work.

Return of
Deposit

8.2 The Vendor shall thereupon return the Deposit to the Purchaser without deduction and without interest save that he shall be entitled to retain such part of the Deposit as shall be necessary to defray any boatyard or surveyor's charges not paid by the Purchaser.

Neither party shall thereafter have any claim against the other under this agreement.

Warranties 9. The Vendor being a person not selling the Yacht in the course of a business, and the Purchaser being at liberty to inspect the Yacht and satisfy himself as to her condition and specification, all express or implied warranties or conditions, statutory or otherwise, are hereby excluded and the Yacht, her outfit, gear and equipment shall be taken with all defects and faults of description without any allowance or abatement whatsoever.

Risk 10. Until the Yacht has been accepted or shall be deemed to have been accepted by the Purchaser she shall be at the risk of the Vendor who shall make good all damage sustained by her before the date of acceptance. If the Yacht be lost or becomes a constructive total loss before such acceptance, this agreement shall be null and void except that the Purchaser will be liable for the cost of all work authorised by him under Clauses 4 and 8 and undertaken before such loss took place and the Deposit shall be returned to the Purchaser without interest but less any deduction made under Clauses 4 and 8 and otherwise without deduction and the Purchaser shall have no claim against the Vendor for damages or otherwise. After acceptance the Yacht shall in all respects be at the risk of the Purchaser.

Notwithstanding the provisions of this clause the ownership of the Yacht will not vest in the Purchaser until payment of the balance of the Purchase Price in accordance with Clause 7 even though the Purchaser may have insured his risk under the provisions of this clause.

Default by Purchaser 11.1 Should the Purchaser fail to pay the balance of the Purchase Price in accordance with Clause 7, the Vendor may give notice in writing to the Purchaser requiring him to complete the purchase within fourteen days of the service of such notice.

If the Purchaser fails to comply with the notice then the Vendor may re-sell the Yacht by public auction or private treaty and any deposit paid shall thereupon be forfeit without prejudice to the

Vendor's right to claim from the Purchaser the amount of any loss on re-sale together with all his reasonable costs and expenses, due allowance being made for any forfeited deposit. On the expiry of the said notice the Yacht shall be at the Vendor's risk.

Default by Vendor

11.2 If the Vendor shall default in the execution of his part of the contract the Purchaser shall, without prejudice to any other rights he may have hereunder, be entitled to the return of the Deposit.

Unless such default by the Vendor shall have arisen from events over which the Vendor had no control, the Vendor shall pay interest upon the amount of the Deposit for the period during which he has held it at the rate of 4% per annum above finance house base rate, together with compensation for any loss which the Purchaser may have sustained as a result of the Vendor's default.

Arbitration

12. All disputes that cannot be resolved between the Parties and which arise out of or in connection with this agreement shall be submitted to a single arbitrator to be appointed, in default of agreement, by the Chairman of the Council of the RYA and the provisions of the Arbitration Act 1950 (as amended) shall apply.

Notices

13. Any notice under this agreement shall be in writing and any notice to the Purchaser or Vendor shall be sufficiently served if delivered to him personally or posted by recorded delivery to his last known address. Any notice posted shall be deemed to have been received forty eight hours after the time of posting and any notice given in any other manner shall be deemed to have been received at the time when, in the ordinary course of post, it may be expected to have been received.

Jurisdiction

14. This agreement shall be construed according to and governed by the Law of England (or of Scotland if the Vendor's address shall be in that country) and the Parties hereby submit to the jurisdiction of the Courts of the same countries.

Marginal notes

15. The construction of this agreement is not to be affected by any marginal notes.

Entire agreement

16. This agreement forms the entire agreement between the Parties unless otherwise specifically agreed in writing between them.

SIGNED BY THE VENDOR
In the presence of :

SIGNED BY THE PURCHASER
In the presence of :

AGREEMENT FOR CONSTRUCTION OF A NEW CRAFT

DATE OF AGREEMENT   19

PARTIES
(Insert full names and address)

1 'The Builders' :
of

2 'The Purchaser' :
of

These terms include successors in title

PRICE * £   , payable as follows :
(a) Upon the signing of this agreement   £
(b) Upon the hull being available at the Builders'
      premises, fully moulded, planked, plated or formed £
(c) Upon substantial completion of the fitting of the
      interior joinery work, installation of the engine
      or stepping of the mast, whichever is the earlier   £
(d) Upon completion of an acceptance trial, and the
      signing of the satisfaction note by the Purchaser
      or his agent (see Clause 7)   £

* N.B.

● **VAT.** Where VAT is payable, it forms part of the price. The figures on this page must therefore include VAT at the rate applicable at the date of the agreement. The Government has power to alter VAT rates and classifications : any such alterations would bind both parties and be reflected in instalment payments under this agreement.

● **Instalments.** It is suggested that instalment (a) above should normally be not more than 20% of the total price, except that it should be not more than 30% in cases where the Builders are buying in the hull or ordering the engines at an early stage. It is also suggested that instalment (d) should be not less than 10% of the total price.

These figures are no more than a guide and may be varied by agreement between the parties.

DELIVERY (see Clause 4)
Expected Date :   19
Place :

ACCEPTANCE TRIAL (see Clause 7.1)
Maximum duration :   hours
Place :

AGREEMENT : The Builders will build and the Purchaser will buy a craft,
subject to the within-written terms of this agreement.

SIGNED by the Builders
in the presence of :
(Witness)

SIGNED by the Purchaser
in the presence of :
(Witness)

SATISFACTION NOTE
(For signature after acceptance trial – see Clause 7.3)

I, the undersigned, hereby certify that the construction of the craft and the
acceptance trial have been completed to my reasonable satisfaction.
     This satisfaction note will not affect my statutory rights should the craft
or its equipment later prove to be defective (see Clause 8).

Dated :   19

SIGNED :
Signature of Purchaser or his agent

Terms of agreement

Specification
1.   The Builders will build and the Purchaser will buy the craft ('the
      craft') described in the specification and drawings ('the specification')
      annexed to this agreement. The Builders will construct the craft in
      compliance with the specification. The Purchaser and/or his autho-
      rised agent shall have the right to reject all workmanship, materials
      and/or equipment which is not in compliance with the requirements
      set out in the specification. Such rejection shall be ineffective unless
      confirmed promptly to the Builders in writing in accordance with
      Clause 15.

Modifications or additions
2.   Any modification or additions to the specification shall not form part
      of this agreement until confirmed by both parties in writing.

Price and instalments
3.1   The price of the craft, and the stages at which it shall be paid by the
      Purchaser to the Builders, shall be as stated at the commencement of
      this agreement.

Price variation clause (see note 7)

3.2 If so required by the Builders, the price stated shall be increased by the addition thereto of such percentage of each instalment (other than the first) as is equal to the percentage increase in the figure at which the Index of Retail Prices stands at the date upon which the instalment falls due over the figure at which the Index stood at the date of this agreement. Further, the Builders may require the Purchaser to pay any increased costs resulting from a change in law or regulation occurring or announced between the date of this agreement and the final instalment falling due. However :

(a) no account shall be taken of increases in the price which would not have been chargeable but for the failure of the Builders to proceed with the construction of the craft with reasonable despatch;

(b) if there is a material change in the basis of compiling the Index of Retail Prices published by the Department of Employment (or by any government department upon which duties in connection with the Index shall have devolved) or if that Index is discontinued, price adjustments shall be based on some other index to be agreed from time to time by the BMIF and the RYA;

(c) to the extent that the Builders do not make an increase when demanding an earlier instalment, the entire amount of the increase shall be payable with the final instalment.

Delivery date and place

4.1 The Builders shall deliver the craft, completed in compliance with the specification, to the Purchaser or his agent by the date and at the place stated in this agreement, but subject to prior signature of the satisfaction note herein. This delivery date shall be deferred if completion is delayed due to modifications or additions to the specification or any cause whatsoever (including delay by suppliers in delivering equipment) outside the control of the Builders.

4.2 If all or any of the materials or equipment built in to the craft or appropriated to this agreement shall be seriously damaged by any cause whatever, the delivery date stated herein shall be deferred for such time as is necessary for the Builders to reinstate the work and to purchase and obtain delivery of materials or equipment in substitution for those damaged.

Agreed damages clause

This clause may be added to the printed form of agreement for construction of a new craft if it is of great importance to the Purchaser that the craft should be delivered by the date specified.

The figure to be inserted in the blank space should not be in the nature of a penalty, and may be subject to an agreed maximum. It should be a genuine pre-estimate of the loss likely to be caused to the Purchaser by the delay. The figure might well be based on the cost of chartering a comparable craft.

AGREED DAMAGES CLAUSE

If due to the Builders' failure without reasonable cause to proceed with reasonable despatch, the craft is not completed by the date set out above (as deferred under sub-clause 4.2 where necessary) and if the Purchaser has not exercised his rights under clause 5, the Builders shall pay the Purchaser * £......... in respect of each week or part of a week until the craft is completed as agreed damages for his loss of use of the craft.

Insert initials of both parties

....

Builders' failure to proceed
5.   If the Builders fail without reasonable cause to proceed with the construction of the craft with reasonable despatch, the Purchaser shall be at liberty to remove the craft and such materials and equipment as have been purchased or appropriated by the Builders for construction of the craft, provided that payments made or tendered by the Purchaser to the Builders are at least equivalent to the cost to the Builders of the goods to be removed (including the Builders' current profit margins). If the craft is at such a stage of construction that it is impracticable to remove it, the Purchaser shall be entitled to employ alternative labour and materials to proceed with the construction of the craft (and to exercise all necessary rights of access to the Builders' premises during their normal business hours), but only as far as is necessary to enable the craft to be removed. Such rights shall be without prejudice to any other rights that the Purchaser may have.

Access to craft and Builders' premises
6.   Subject to the prior consent of the Builders, the Purchaser and/or his authorised agent shall have free and reasonable access to the craft and to the materials and equipment to be used in the craft, for the purpose of inspection at any time during the normal business hours of the Builders' establishment. Such consent shall not be unreasonably withheld but may be granted on terms that the Purchaser or his agent is accompanied by a representative of the Builders. Such right of access shall extend only to those parts of the Builders' premises necessary for the purpose of such inspection. If the Purchaser or his agent shall for that or any other purpose use any part of the Builders' premises and/or facilities, and whether by invitation or otherwise, he shall do so at his own risk, unless any injury or damage to person or property is caused by or results from the negligence or any deliberate act of the Builders or of those for whom they are responsible.

Acceptance trial
7.1 Not less than twenty eight days in advance (unless a shorter time be agreed by the parties), the Builders shall notify the Purchaser in writ-

ing that the craft will be ready for an acceptance trial on a stated date. The Purchaser or his authorised agent shall present himself within seven days after that date, at an agreed time, to accompany the Builders or their representative upon an acceptance trail lasting not more than the duration stated in this agreement (such acceptance trial to be at the Builders' expense). If the Purchaser or his authorised agent shall fail to so present himself, then at the end of such seven day period, the acceptance trial shall be deemed to have taken place.

7.2   If at the end of such acceptance trial the Purchaser or his agent shall for good cause refuse to accept the craft until faults have been rectified, then the Builders shall rectify the same, and if necessary a second trial shall be held in accordance with the provisions of sub-clause 7.1.

7.3   At the satisfactory conclusion of the acceptance trial or, as the case may be, after satisfactory rectification of any faults, the Purchaser or his agent shall sign the satisfaction note contained in this agreement. The final instalment shall become payable immediately upon signature of such note or upon unreasonable failure or refusal to sign. If the Purchaser or his agent shall fail to present himself within the seven days period mentioned in sub-clause 7.1, the final instalment shall become payable at the end of such period.

7.4   If the Purchaser shall fail to take delivery of the craft within twenty eight days of the final instalment falling due, the Builders may thereafter require him to pay reasonable mooring or storage charges until he does so.

Statutory rights of Purchaser (see note 8)
8.   The craft and all materials and equipment are supplied with the benefit of the undertakings (particularly as to conformity of goods with description or sample, and as to their quality or fitness for a particular purpose) which are implied by the Sale of Goods Act 1979. Nothing in this agreement shall affect those statutory rights.

Insurance (see note 9)
9.   The craft and all materials and equipment supplied or installed by the Builders which are from time to time intended for the craft and within the premises of the Builders shall be insured by them. Such insurance shall be at Lloyd's or with an insurance company belonging to the British Insurance Association, against all Builders' Risks in accordance with 'Institute Clauses for Builders' Risks amended for Yacht and Motor Boat' until delivery. In the event of the craft, equipment or materials sustaining damage at any time before delivery, any monies received in respect of the insurance shall be applied by the Builders in making good the damage during ordinary working hours in a reasonable and workmanlike manner. However, if the Builders cannot reasonably be expected to make good such damage, then unless this agreement is determined under sub-clause 10.1 or 10.2 they shall pay to the Purchaser the monies so received (but not so as

to exceed the instalments then paid by the Purchaser). The Purchaser shall not on account of the said damage or repair be entitled to reject or to make any objection to the craft, equipment or materials, or to make any claim in respect of any resultant depreciation in its or their value or utility.

The insurance liability of the Builders under this clause shall cease upon delivery of the craft to the Purchaser.

Termination of agreement in event of damage

10.1 Notwithstanding the foregoing, the Builders may in their discretion elect either to fulfil or to determine this agreement if from any cause (other than the negligence or any deliberate act of the Builders or of those for whom they are responsible) and at any time :

(a) the craft shall become a total loss or be deemed to be a constructive, arranged or compromised total loss, or

(b) the Builders' premises, plant, machinery, equipment or any of them shall be seriously damaged so as to make it impracticable for the Builders to complete the craft.

If the Builders shall elect to determine this agreement, they shall forthwith refund to the Purchaser any instalments of the purchase price received by them. This agreement will thereupon be determined in all respects as if it had been duly completed and the Purchaser shall have no further right to claim on the Builders.

10.2 If by reason of serious damage to the Builders' premises, plant or machinery, or to the craft, its equipment or the materials intended for it, the craft cannot be delivered within a reasonable time after the delivery date stated herein (as deferred under sub-clause 4.2 where necessary), the Purchaser may determine this agreement. The Builders shall thereupon refund to the Purchaser any instalments of the purchase price received by them and thereupon this agreement will be determined in all respects and neither party shall have any further right to claim on the other.

Passing of property in craft etc

11. The craft and/or all materials and equipment purchased or appropriated from time to time by the Builders specifically for its construction (whether in their premises, water or elsewhere) shall become the property of the Purchaser upon the payment of the first instalment under this agreement or (if it be later) upon the date of the said purchase or appropriation. The Builders shall, however, have a lien upon the craft, materials and equipment for recovery of all sums due (whether invoiced or not) under the terms of this agreement or any variation or modification thereof. Any materials or equipment rejected by the Purchaser shall forthwith re-vest in the Builders.

Unpaid instalments

12. If any instalment shall remain unpaid for twenty eight days after notice has been given to the Purchaser by registered or recorded delivery post, the Builders shall be entitled to interest at 3% above the

Bank of England's base rate for the time being (calculated from the date when the Builders first issued an invoice or other written request for payment of the instalment). After a further period of twenty eight days the Builders shall be at liberty to sell the craft as it then lies, or may complete and sell the craft after completion. On such re-sale the Purchaser shall be refunded any instalments previously paid, subject to deduction therefrom of any loss suffered by the Builders on the re-sale.

Copyright etc
13. Any copyright or similar protection in all drawings, specifications and plans prepared by the Builders or their architects shall remain the property of the Builders.

Bankruptcy etc of Purchaser
14. The Builders shall have the right to terminate this agreement by notice in writing in the event of the Purchaser becoming bankrupt or entering into any composition or arrangement with his creditors or if, being a company, it shall enter into liquidation (otherwise than for the purpose of amalgamation or reconstruction) or any arrangement with its creditors, or shall have a receiver appointed of the whole or any part of its property.

Notices
15. Subject to Clause 12, notices may be given by being handed to the addressee or sent by first class post, telex, cable or telegram to his address as shown in this Agreement (unless the addressee has by written notice to the other party substituted a different address in England as the notice address). Any notice posted shall be deemed to have been received 48 hours after the time of posting and any notice given in any other manner shall be deemed to have been received at the time when in the ordinary course it may be expected to have been received. In proving service of any notice it shall be sufficient to prove that delivery was made or that the envelope containing the notice was properly addressed and posted or that the telex, cable or telegram was properly addressed and sent (as the case may be).

Arbitration
16. All disputes arising out of or in connection with this agreement shall be submitted to a single arbitrator to be appointed, in default of agreement, by the President of the SBBNF and the Chairman of the Council of the RYA and the provisions of the Arbitration Acts 1950 to 1979 shall apply.

Miscellaneous
17.1 This agreement shall be construed according to and governed by the law of England.

17.2 The construction of this agreement is not to be affected by any marginal note.

17.3 Subject always to the statutory rights of the Purchaser, this agreement forms the entire agreement between the parties and, unless specifically agreed in writing by the Builders, no warranty, condition, description or representation is given or to be implied by anything said or written in the negotiations between the parties or their representatives prior to this agreement.

17.4 Reference to any statutory provision includes a reference to that provision as amended, extended or re-enacted and to any statutory replacement thereof (either before or after the date of this agreement).

Additional terms
18. This agreement is subject also to the special terms (if any) set out below, or attached to this agreement and signed by both parties.

Notes

These are explanatory notes only and, although very important, do not form part of the agreement itself.

1. This form is published by the British Marine Industries Federation (BMIF) and approved by the Royal Yachting Association (RYA) and is available from both organisations.

2. It is a simple form of agreement and cannot be expected to cater for every unforeseen circumstance arising between the parties. It does attempt to define the intentions of the parties and is considered by the RYA and the BMIF to hold a reasonable balance between the purchaser and the builders.

3. It should be completed in duplicate, taking care to insert the appropriate details. Any specification, drawing, or additional clause which cannot be accommodated should be firmly attached to the agreement and signed by both parties. Additional clauses should be initialled by both parties.

4. Both parties should sign in the presence of a witness.

5. The satisfaction note must be signed by the purchaser or his agent on delivery of the completed craft.

6. If it is of great importance to the purchaser that the craft should be delivered by the date specified, a suitable 'agreed damages clause' for attachment to the agreement is available from the SBBNF and RYA.

7. (a) Clause 3.2 is a price variation clause which allows the builders to

adjust the price to reflect inflation occurring between the dates of the agreement and the final instalment falling due. The clause should be deleted where the parties agree on a 'fixed-price contract' (usually where the period between signing and final payment is likely to be short).

(b) Builders are reminded that the clause does not permit a price increase to reflect inflation occurring between original quotation and signature of the agreement. For this reason builders should express their quotations as valid for a limited period and, if necessary, should revise them where the agreement is signed after that period.

(c) The clause allows builders to increase the price so as to reflect all increases in the Retail Prices Index occurring after the date of the agreement. If they intend to rely on the clause, builders should base the price on current costs without the addition of any inflation factor.

8. If any defect should be discovered in the craft or its equipment after the purchaser has taken delivery, it will be in his own interests to give immediate written notice to the builders in accordance with Clause 15. If a builder is to be legally liable to rectify the defect, it must usually be shown that the defect arises from a breach of this agreement or of the undertakings implied at the time of the sale by the Sale of Goods Act 1983 as amended.

This note does not affect the purchaser's statutory rights.

9. If the purchaser leaves or arranges for others to leave any items on the builders' premises or on the craft, he should insure the item himself unless the builders expressly agree in writing to do so. However, builders should have adequate insurance cover against claims arising from their negligence which result in damage to any property on their premises.

10. Copies of this agreement may be obtained from: British Marine Industries Federation, Meadlake Place, Thorpe Lea Road, Egham, Surrey TW20 8HE or The Royal Yachting Association, RYA House, Romsey Road, Eastleigh, Hampshire SO5 4YA.

AGREEMENT FOR THE BAREBOAT CHARTER OF A PLEASURE CRAFT

AN AGREEMENT made the   day of   19

BETWEEN :
of   ('the Owner')

and
of   ('the Hirer')

In respect of the charter of the UN/REGISTERED PLEASURE CRAFT

Name :
Description :

including all equipment, machinery and gear on board ('the Yacht') and any specific inventory attached hereto initialled by both parties and forming part of this agreement.

DEFINITIONS

'Charter Period'	:	from hours on	19
		to hours on	19
'Cruising Limits'	:	the area bounded by	
'Charter Fee'	:	the sum of £	
'Advance Payment'	:	the sum of £	
'Balance of Charter Fee' :		the sum of £	
'Security Deposit'	:	the sum of £	
'Owner' and 'Hirer'	:	shall include the persons named above and their respective successors in title.	

WHEREBY IT IS AGREED AS FOLLOWS :

1. CHARTER AND ADVANCE PAYMENT

Agreement
to let

The Owner shall let and the Hirer shall charter the Yacht for the Charter Period for the Charter Fee. The Advance Payment shall be paid to the Owner on the signing of this agreement. The Balance of the Charter Fee, and the Security Deposit, shall be paid to the Owner in cash or banker's draft at least fourteen days before the start of the Charter Period.

2. SECURITY DEPOSIT

The Hirer shall pay the Security Deposit to the Owner as security against the Yacht not being returned in good condition and towards any loss of or damage to the Yacht occurring during the Charter Period which is the responsibility of the Hirer under Clause 5.3 and against any loss or damage suffered by the Owner due to any breach of this agreement by the Hirer but without prejudice to any claim over and above the Security Deposit which the Owner may have.

The Security Deposit or any balance remaining shall be returned to the Hirer within fourteen days after re-delivery of the Yacht to the Owner or, in the case of dispute, upon the determination of that dispute.

3. DELIVERY OF YACHT

3.1 Before the start of the Charter Period the Hirer shall have the opportunity to inspect the Yacht in company with the Owner or his agent for the purpose of ensuring that the Yacht and its equipment are in proper working order and further shall have the right to insist on a trail of at least one hour's duration.   Acceptance of the Yacht shall imply (prima facie) that the Yacht is in good order.

Hirer's competence

Likewise the Owner shall have the right to insist that the Hirer and at least one member of his party accompany the Owner for trials to establish to the satisfaction of the Owner their ability to handle the Yacht unattended in the Cruising Limits.

Hirer's failure to accept delivery

3.2 If the Hirer shall fail to accept delivery of the Yacht within forty eight hours from the start of the Charter Period and shall not have notified the Owner of his intention to accept delivery later during the Charter Period, then the Owner shall be at liberty to treat this agreement as determined. The Owner's rights upon termination shall be set out in Clause 7.1, the Hirer shall, however, be given credit for any sum recovered by the Owner if he succeeds in re-letting the Yacht in accordance with the conditions set out in Clause 7.3.

4. OBLIGATIONS OF THE OWNER

The Owner hereby UNDERTAKES as follows :

Owner's
duty on
hand-over
of Yacht

4.1 To use his best endeavours to hand over the Yacht to the Hirer at the start of the Charter Period in full commission, fully bunkered (subject) to Clause 4.3) in good condition and with all the necessary gear and equipment, including any items specified in the inventory and any tools and equipment necessary for minor foreseeable repairs. The Owner does not warrant the fitness of the Yacht in all conditions of weather for any particular cruise or passage within the Cruising Limits.

Refund by
Owner in
case of
delay or
inability
to deliver

4.2 To use his best endeavours to deliver the Yacht to the Hirer at the agreed time and place. If for any cause the Yacht shall not be so delivered then, subject to Clause 3.2, a pro rata refund shall be made to the Hirer for each complete twelve hours' delay. If the delay should exceed forty eight hours, this agreement shall become null and void and the Owner shall return to the Hirer the Advance Payment, the proportion of the Charter Fee already paid and the Security Deposit in full, but without further liability for either party to pay compensation to the other.

Fuelling

4.3 To use his best endeavours to hand over the Yacht at the start of the Charter Period in a fully bunkered condition, but if he is unable to do so then he shall agree with the Hirer upon handover the levels of usable fuel, lubricating oil, water and other similar stores.

Provision
of
documentation

4.4 To obtain and provide any necessary documentation for the Yacht in accordance with the regulations for the time being in force under the Customs and Excise or other Acts and any amending statute, and to assist the Hirer to ensure that the Yacht is provided with the necessary ship's papers.

5. OBLIGATIONS OF THE HIRER

In addition to the obligations of the Hirer in respect of insurance in Clause 6 the Hirer UNDERTAKES as follows :

Take-over
of stores
etc

5.1 If at the commencement of the Charter Period the Yacht is handed over in a fully bunkered condition, to return the Yacht at the end of the Charter Period in the same condition. In other circumstances it shall be the Owner's obligation to agree with the Hirer the present levels of all usable fuel, lubricating oil, water and other similar consumable stores at the commencement of the Charter Period and the Hirer shall be responsible for ensuring that the Yacht is returned at the end of the Charter Period similarly bunkered. In the event that the Hirer does not fulfil this obligation a difference in levels shall be agreed between the Owner and the Hirer at the end of the Charter Period and the cost of the difference shall be deducted from the Security Deposit.

Payment of running expenses

5.2 To pay for all running expenses during the Charter Period, including the cost of charts (if not supplied), food, laundry charges, water, fuel, bills of health, harbour dues, port dues, pilotage, victuals and provisions for himself and his party.

Reparation for loss or damage

5.3 With the exception of loss or damage arising from latent defects or from fair wear and tear, to make good all loss of or damage to any stores, gear, equipment or furnishings of every kind belonging to the Yacht caused during the Charter Period which is not recoverable under the Insurance effected by the Owner as well as any loss or damage arising after the Charter Period but attributable to any act or default of the Hirer or any member of his party.

Hirer's duty to report accidents or damage

5.4 To report to the Owner (and, where applicable to the insurers) as soon as possible any event likely to give rise to a claim under the insurance and any other accident, damage or failure of or to the Yacht, and to comply with any reasonable instructions given to him by the Owner of the insurers.

The Hirer shall use his best endeavours to obtain the approval of the Owner, and shall obtain a written estimate for any work likely to cost over £50, before putting any repairs in hand.

Agreement not to sub-let

5.5 Not to lend, sub-let or otherwise part with control of the Yacht.

Restriction of user

5.6 Not to use the Yacht for any purpose other than private pleasure cruising for himself, his crew and his guests, not to race the Yacht without the prior consent of the Owner. The Hirer further undertakes not to tow any dinghy but to lash it on deck.

Maximum number of persons on board

5.7 To limit the number of his party to not more than the number of berths on the Yacht unless the Owner grants permission for a greater number.

Cruising Limits	5.8	Not to take the Yacht outside the Cruising Limits.
Unlawful acts	5.9	Not knowingly or recklessly to permit to be done or to do or fail to do any act which may render void the Owner's policy of insurance or result in the forfeiture of the Yacht.
Indemnity by Hirer in cases where yacht insurance becomes void	5.10	If the insurance policy of the Yacht shall be rendered void or the policy monies withheld in whole or in part by reason of any act or default of the Hirer or any member of his party, the Hirer hereby agrees to indemnify the Owner against any loss consequent upon such act or default.
Duty of care in regard to safety and security	5.11	To be fully responsible for the safety and security of the Yacht at all times during the Charter Period. Unless the Yacht is moored or anchored in a harbour, marina or similar location, he further undertakes that the Yacht shall at no time be left unattended and at least one member of the party shall remain on board in such circumstances.
Observation of regulations	5.12	To observe all regulations of Customs, Port, Harbour or other Authorities to which the Yacht becomes subject.
No animals on board	5.13	At no time during the Charter Period to allow any animals on board the Yacht.
Customs clearance	5.14	To ensure that the Yacht is properly cleared by British Customs on leaving for and returning from abroad.

6. INSURANCE AND LIABILITIES

Yacht insurance	6.1	The Owner shall insure the Yacht for its full market value against fire and all the usual marine and collision risks with protection and indemnity cover of at least £1,000,000 (but not so as to cover the first £50.00 of any claim, or damage to sails unless caused by a dismasting or collision). The Owner also undertakes to inform the appropriate broker or underwriter that the Yacht is on charter to the Hirer for the Charter Period. The Owner will provide for the Hirer on request a copy of the policy or certificate and shall ensure that the Hirer is covered under the policy or certificate for the same risks as the Owner himself.
	6.2	The Owner shall not, however, be liable for any personal injury, or any loss of, or damage to, the personal property of the Hirer or any member of

his party, or any other person invited aboard the Yacht by the Hirer during the Charter Period.

6.3   Should major damage occur to the Yacht during the Charter Period so as to involve a claim on the policy of insurance as described in Clause 6.1 or should a major breakdown of the gear or machinery occur of a nature to make the Yacht unseaworthy, a pro rata refund will be made for the period during which the Yacht was unseaworthy, PROVIDED ALWAYS that neither the Hirer nor any member of his party caused or contributed to the damage or breakdown.

6.4   Notwithstanding anything in this agreement the Hirer shall not be entitled to claim from the Owner any other compensation in respect of damage or breakdown or of any consequential loss however caused.

6.5   If the Yacht shall become an actual or constructive total loss during the Charter Period then provided that the insurance of the Yacht has not been rendered void or the policy monies withheld in whole or in part by reason of any act or default of the Hirer or any member of his party this agreement shall terminate and the Security Deposit and the pro rata proportion of the Charter Fee shall be repaid to the Hirer.

7. TERMINATION OF AGREEMENT

Hirer's
failure
to pay
or comply
with terms
of
agreement

7.1   If any payment due under this agreement is not made on or by the appointed day, or if the Hirer fails to comply with any other provision in this agreement, the Owner may forthwith terminate this agreement and resume possession of the Yacht, but without prejudice to the right of the Owner to recover any unpaid part of the Charter Fee and damages in respect of any breach of this agreement by the Hirer.

Notice of
withdrawal
more than
two months
prior to
commencement

7.2   If the Hirer gives written notice to the Owner more than two calendar months before the start of the Charter Period that the Yacht will not be required, no liability for the Balance of the Charter Fee will remain (and if it and/or the Security Deposit have already been paid then it and/or they shall be refunded by the Owner to the Hirer), but the Advance Payment shall be forfeit except that 50% will be refunded if the Owner re-lets the yacht for the Charter Period at the same or a greater charter fee. In such circumstances the Owner agrees to use his best endeavours to re-let the Yacht.

Notice of withdrawal within two months of commencement of Charter Period

7.3 If the Hirer gives notice to the Owner within two calendar months before the start of the Charter Period that the Yacht will not be required, then the Owner will use his best endeavours to re-let the Yacht and the following provisions shall apply :

7.3.1 If the Owner is unable to re-let the Yacht, then the Hirer remains fully liable for all payments due under this agreement;

7.3.2 If the Owner is able to do so at the same or a greater charter fee, then the Hirer's liability shall be limited to 50% of the Advance Payment;

7.3.3 If the Owner is only able to do so at less than the Charter Fee, then the Hirer will be liable for the difference between the net sum which the Owner receives and the payments due under this agreement.

8. RE-DELIVERY OF THE YACHT

Hirer's responsibility upon re-delivery

8.1 The Hirer will re-deliver the Yacht to the Owner free of indebtedness at the end of the Charter Period in as good, clean and tidy condition as when delivered to the Hirer (fair wear and tear excepted), at the Yacht's base or other mutually convenient place to be notified to the Hirer.

Penalty for late return of Yacht

8.2 If the Hirer shall fail to re-deliver the Yacht the time and place agreed, he shall be liable to pay to the owner the sum of £[ ] for every day or part of a day by which re-delivery is delayed unless the delay is caused by the operation of a peril covered by the terms of the policy or certificate of insurance referred to in clause 6.1 hereof or by such damage to, or failure of, the Yacht as may have been reported to the Owner under Clause 5.4.

9. SETTLEMENT OF DISPUTES

In the event of any dispute arising out of this agreement such shall be referred to a sole arbitrator whose decision shall be final. If the parties are unable to agree on the nomination of an arbitrator then he shall be nominated by the Chairman of the Council of the RYA.

10. LAW

This agreement shall be governed by English Law.

11. MARGINAL NOTES

The Explanatory marginal notes shall not affect the meaning of nor form part of this agreement.

SIGNED BY THE OWNER
in the presence of :

SIGNED BY THE HIRER
in the presence of :

AGREEMENT FOR THE SYNDICATE OWNERSHIP OF A YACHT

AN AGREEMENT made the   day of   19

BETWEEN   of

                                                               ('the first owner')

and   of

                                                              ('the second owner')

The owners include their respective successors in title and shall hereinafter be collectively referred to as 'the Parties'.

WHEREAS the Parties wish to enter into an agreement to share the management and use of the yacht '   ' ('the Yacht')

[and WHEREAS the first owner is the present owner of the Yacht]
[and WHEREAS the second owner has by a prior contract purchased from the first owner   /64ths of the Yacht]
[and WHEREAS the Parties have jointly and severally purchased the Yacht in the following shares :

    the first owner purchasing   /64ths

    the second owner purchasing   /64ths

and WHEREAS the parties have jointly and severally entered into an agreement with [   ] (the 'Mortgage Company')].

NOW IT IS HEREBY MUTUALLY AGREED between the Parties as follows:

Joint bank account	1.	The first owner shall forthwith open a [Bank/ Building Society] account ('the Account') in the names of the Parties into which the Parties shall upon the [ ] day of [ ] in each year transfer the amount of £[ ] until six months after the termination of this agreement in accordance with Clause 5.
Withdrawals and . contributions from/to account	2.	The first [and second] owner/s shall have power [jointly/separately] to draw monies from the Account for the sole purpose of the maintenance and management of the Yacht as [he/they] shall in their absolute discretion think fit and shall have power to call for further and necessary contributions in equal shares from [the second owner/each

other] subject always to the safeguards in Clause 4.7 and to the general law affecting principal and agent.

Casual disbursements

3. Any disbursement, payment or account discharged by one owner on behalf of the other and of the general management of the yacht shall from time to time as convenient but certainly once annually be reported to the other owner and each owner jointly and severally agrees to contribute one half of such disbursements, payments or accounts upon proper documentation in the form of receipts etc. being presented as evidence of payment.

Management responsibility

4. The first owner shall have the following powers, duties and responsibilities :

4.1 to make day-to-day decisions for the general management of the Yacht;

4.2 to make (after consultation with the second owner) any arrangement for the purchase of capital equipment such as sails, engines etc. as may be necessary and for any agreement to charter the Yacht;

4.3 to insure the Yacht, her apparel, fittings etc. against the usual risks either at Lloyd's or with an insurance company or association;

4.4 to employ any yard, sail-loft, brokers or agents on their usual terms of business and to transact any necessary business in relation to the Yacht;

4.5 to make, adjust, apportion or settle at his discretion any salvage, damage, average or other claims in favour of or against the Yacht or to refer the same to arbitration;

4.6 to take such steps as may be necessary to defend proceedings, accept service or arrange finance relating to the Yacht;

4.7 as soon as reasonably practicable after the [ ] day of [   ] in each year to render to the second owner accounts paid together with the Account statements as evidence of payment, and on request to produce all vouchers, books or other documents and papers relating to the management of the Account and of the Yacht.

Termination of Agreement

5. If either of the Parties has reasonable cause or desire to terminate this agreement, he may, by individual notice in writing to the other party,

indicate his desire to terminate. Such termination shall take place within six months after the delivery of such notice in writing.

Upon such notice in writing being delivered, the other party shall take such steps as may be necessary to secure the execution of a proper release and indemnity against all liabilities contracted by the determining party and shall arrange to purchase the share of the determining party at a fair market price or alternatively obtain agreement by another to take on the share of the determining party. Likewise, the determining party hereby agrees to defray or settle all his share of the disbursements, payments or accounts for the Yacht up to and including the date of actual termination as agreed between the Parties which for the avoidance of doubt may be any date within six months of the individual notice in writing being received by the other party.

If a dispute arises as to the price to be paid to the determining party for his share then a valuation shall be obtained from a recognised yacht broker and in default of agreement then the entirety of the Yacht shall be publicly advertised for sale with notice of time and place for sale being given to both Parties and she shall be sold. Each of the Parties on receiving his share of the purchase money shall execute the necessary Bill of Sale of his share in the Yacht to the purchaser and deliver up possession of the Yacht. The costs of such sale shall be paid by the Parties according to their respective shares.

6. Where it is agreed to terminate this agreement and the Parties have mutually agreed to sell the Yacht, it shall then be sold either by private treaty at such price as the Parties may agree or, in default of such agreement, by public auction subject to such conditions as are usual on the sale of such yachts. Each of the Parties shall be at liberty to bid for and purchase the Yacht at any such public auction, or to purchase the Yacht outright for the price advertised for sale by private treaty.

Regular
payment of
mortgage etc

7.1 In the case of a mortgage or hire purchase agreement being in operation each owner jointly and severally agrees to pay his monthly or other contribution to defray the costs of such mortgage or hire purchase agreement into the Account in accordance with Clause 1 until the date of determination agreed in accordance with Clause 5.

Final settlement of mortgage debt

7.2   In the event of the sale of the Yacht, each owner jointly and severally agrees with the other to defray from his share of the sale price his share of the mortgage or hire purchase agreement entered into with the Mortgage Company.

Arbitration

8.   If, any dispute, difference or question arises between the Parties relating to the rights, duties or obligations of either of them, including (without prejudice to the generality hereof) any dispute, difference or question whether the owners have, in fact, properly and satisfactorily carried out their obligations under this agreement, the same shall be referred to arbitration by a single arbitrator to be agreed upon by the Parties or, failing such agreement, appointed by the Secretary-General of the RYA. This shall be deemed to be a submission to arbitration within the Arbitration Act 1950.

9.   Any notice under this agreement shall be in writing and shall be sufficiently served if delivered personally or posted to the last known postal address in Great Britain or Ireland of either of the Parties.

IN WITNESS whereof this agreement has been signed by the Parties the day and year first above written

SIGNED BY THE FIRST OWNER ....
in the presence of :

SIGNED BY THE SECOND OWNER ....
in the presence of :

SIMPLE FORM OF SALVAGE AGREEMENT 'NO CURE - NO PAY'

(Incorporating Lloyd's Open Form)

On board the yacht   Date

IT IS HEREBY AGREED BETWEEN

for and on behalf of the Owners of the
(hereinafter called 'the Owners')

AND   for and on behalf of
(hereinafter called 'the Contractor')

1. That the Contractor will use his best endeavours to salve the
and take her into

or such other place as may hereinafter be agreed or if no place is named or
agreed to a place of safety.

2. That the services shall be rendered by the Contractor and accepted by
the owner as salvage services upon the principle of 'No cure - No pay'
subject to the terms, conditions and provisions (including those relating to
Arbitration and the providing of security) of the current Standard Form of
Salvage Agreement approved and published by the Council of Lloyd's of
London and known as Lloyd's Open Form.

3. In the event of success the Contractor's remuneration shall be £... or if
no fixed sum be mutually agreed between the parties or entered herein
same shall be fixed by arbitration in London in the manner prescribed in
Lloyd's Open Form.

4. The Owners, their servants and agents shall cooperate fully with the
Contractor in and about the salvage including obtaining entry to the place
named in Clause 1 hereof or the place of safety. The Contractor may make
reasonable use of the vessel's machinery gear equipment anchors chains
stores and other appurtenances during and for the purpose of the services
free of expense but shall not unnecessarily damage abandon or sacrifice
the same or any property the subject of this Agreement.

For and on behalf of the Owners of property to be salved

....

For and on behalf of the Contractor

....

Note Full copies of the Lloyd's Open Form Salvage Agreement can be obtained from the Salvage Arbitration Branch, Lloyd's of London, One Lime Street, London EC3M 7HA, Tel: (071) 623 7100 Ext 5849, who should be notified of the services only when no agreement can be reached as to remuneration.

USEFUL ADDRESSES

British Marine Industries
Federation,
Meadlake Place,
Thorpe Lea Road,
Egham,
Surrey TW20 8HE
Tel: 0784 473377

British Waterways Board,
Willow Grange,
Church Road,
Watford,
Hertfordshire WD1 3QA
Tel: 0923 226422

Central Council of Physical
Recreation,
Francis House,
Francis Street,
London SW1P 1DE
Tel: 071-828 3163

Cruising Association,
Ivory House,
St Katherines Dock,
London E1 9AT
Tel: 071-481 0881

HM Coastguard,
Department of Transport,
90 High Holborn,
London WC1V 6LP
Tel: 071-405 6911

HM Customs and Excise,
Dorset House,
Stamford Street,
London SE1 9PS
Tel: 071-928 3344

Inland Waterways Association,
114 Regents Park Road,
London NW1 8UQ
Tel: 071-586 2556

Marine Accidents Investigation
Branch,
5/7 Brunswick Place,
Southampton,
Hampshire SO1 2AN
Tel: 0703 232424

Meteorological Office,
London Road,
Bracknell,
Berkshire RG12 2SZ
Tel: 0344 420242

National Rivers Authority,
Head Office,
Rivers House,
Waterside Drive,
Aztec West,
Almondsbury,
Bristol BS12 4UD
Tel: 0454 624400

National Rivers Authority,
Anglian Region,
Kingfisher House,
Goldhay Way,
Orton Goldhay,
Peterborough PE2 0ZR
Tel: 0733 371811

National Rivers Authority,
Southern Region,
Guildbourne House,
Chatsworth Road,
Worthing,
West Sussex BN11 1LD
Tel: 0903 820629

National Rivers Authority,
Thames Region,
Kings Meadow House,
Kings Meadow Road,
Reading RG1 8DQ
Tel: 0734 535000

Radio Communications Agency,
Department of Trade and
    Industry,
Waterloo Bridge House,
Waterloo Road,
London SE1 8UA
Tel: 071-215 5000

Registrar General of Shipping and
    Seamen,
Government Building,
St Agnes Road,
Gabalfa,
Cardiff CF4 4YA
0222 747333

Royal National Lifeboat
    Institution,
West Quay Road,
Poole,
Dorset BH15 1HZ
Tel: 0202 671133

Royal Ocean Racing Club,
20 St James's Place,
London SW1A 1NN
Tel: 071-493 3871

Royal Yachting Association,
RYA House,
Romsey Road,
Eastleigh,
Hampshire SO5 4YA
Tel: 0703 629962

Small Ships Register,
DVLA,
Swansea SA99 1BX
Tel: 0792 783355

Trinity House,
4th Floor,
Lloyd's Chambers,
1 Portsoken Street,
London E1 8BT
Tel: 071-480 6601

Yacht Brokers, Designers &
Surveyors Association,
Wheel House,
Petersfield Road,
Whitehill,
Bordon,
Hampshire GU35 9BU
Tel: 0420 473862

Yacht Charter Association,
60 Silverdale,
New Milton,
Hampshire BH25 7DE
Tel: 0425 619004

INDEX

ABYA 15, 50
acceptance of yacht 17, 31
access to yacht 18
Admiralty Warrants 90
agents, buying through 35
anchor, the right to 76–78
antifouling paints 150
arbitration 19, 61, 62, 109

Bathing Water Directive 152
berth leasing 139
　security of tenure 139
　service charges 139
　sub-letting of berths 139
BMIF 28, 34, 35, 50, 62
Board of Trade 64
British Ports Federation 132
British Standards Institute 41
British Transport Commission 86
British Waterways Board 39, 40, 86
Broads Authority 39, 40, 87
builders' certificates 14, 18
Bureau Veritas 45
buying
　deposit 16
　new yacht 28
　second-hand yacht 14, 15
buying for overseas delivery 36

canals, public rights of navigation 86
Caveat Emptor 18, 53
Certificate of Registry 25
Coast Protection Act 1949 78
coastal zone management 81
collision law 64–75
collision regulations 64
commercial waterways 86
compensation, principles of 72
completion of contract 17, 24
Compliance, Certificate of 42
conservation 81
construction and equipment
　regulations 39

Consumer Credit Act 1974 58
Consumer Protection Act 1987 59
contract for buying new yacht 36
contract for sale of second-hand yacht
　15
contributory negligence 69
courts
　county 60, 62
　European 7
　high 10, 25, 44, 60, 62
Crown Estate 140, 141
Crown, title to seabed 76
Crown Estate Commissioners 78, 128,
　140, 141
cruising waterways 86
customs 37
　notice of arrival 37
　notice of departure 146

damages, award of 62, 72
Defence, Ministry of 82, 90
defences to negligence 68
delivery of new yacht 30
Department of Trade and Industry 145
deposit 30
description, sale by 53
docks 76
Duchy of Cornwall 128, 141
Duchy of Lancaster 141

EC Small Craft Directive 48
English Nature 81, 82
ensigns 10, 89, 90, 92
environmental bodies 81
European Boating Association 49
European Community 7, 47, 89, 144,
　146, 152, 153
European Court 7
exhaust emissions 151

fault, proof of 68
flag law 89–94
　Blue Ensign 90–92

national colours 145
Red Ensign 90–92
White Ensign 90–92
foreign cruising 144–148
    documentation 144
    driving licences 147
    flags 145
    insurance 145
    rabies 147
Fundus, ownership of 122, 140
    rent 140
    title by adverse possession 140

garbage, disposal regulations 149
Geneva Convention on the High Seas 2, 10, 89
gunnery range byelaws 82

Harbour Authority, functions of 79, 123
    harbour dues 128
    lifting bridges 130
    natural harbour 131
    powers to regulate activities 124
    private harbour 131
    provision of facilities 127
    provision of moorings 128
harbour law 122–134
Harbour Master's powers 122

inland waters, construction and
    equipment regulations 39
insolvency of builder 31
insurance 95–110
    accidental damage 100
    arbitration 109
    British Waterways Board 95
    claims 107–109
    exclusion clauses 104
    express terms 101
    going foreign 145
    houseboat, use of yacht as 102
    implied terms 99
    Institute Yacht clauses 102
    insurable interest 96, 102
    marinas 95
    passing of risk 18, 31
    perils of the seas 104
    period of commission 102
    policy 98
    proposal form 97
    sails 105
    speedboat clauses 104
    theft 106
    third party cover 106
    total loss 109
    trailing 154

valuations 72, 96
vehicle 154
International Maritime Organisation 65
International Standards Organisation 48, 49
International Yacht Racing Rules 67, 71, 72
inventory 16, 29

Jet-ski 3, 49, 127

Lakes, Public Right of Navigation on 87
Lake District Special Planning Board 87
lifting bridges 130
liability, limitation of 73–75, 95
licences for boat drivers 147
lien, salvage 15
light dues 132
limitation, 2 year period of 2
    title by adverse possession 78
limitation of liability 73–75, 95
Lloyd's 21
Lloyd's Open Form Salvage Agreement 116, 119
Lloyds Insurance 98
load lines 43, 44
local authority planning 79
low water mark 80

Marine Conservation Society 81
marine nature reserves 80, 82
market value (insurance) 72
marking, registration 8
    SSR 11
Marpol Convention 149
marinas 135–140
    access for external workers 137
    berth holders' associations 135
    commercial activities 138
    commission on sale of yacht 136
    contracts 135, 137
    leasing a berth 138
    requirement to insure 95
    sub-letting berths 137
    traffic 79
    work on yacht in marinas 137
Ministry of Agriculture Fisheries and Food 150
Ministry of Defence 82, 128
Misrepresentation Act 1967 54, 55
Moorings 140–143
    rating 142
    rent 140
    right to moor 76–78
    title by adverse possession 78, 140
    trespass 78

Mortgage 5, 12, 22
mussel fisheries 82

National Rivers Authority 39, 40, 151
National Trust 85
nationality of ship 89
nature reserves 80
navigation, public rights of 76–88
negligence 66, 68
    contributory 69
noise, engine 151

overseas delivery, buying for 36
ownership, defined 1
    part/joint 4
Oyster Fisheries 82–83

Passenger Certificate (DTp) 40
pilotage 132, 133
planning authority 79, 80
pollution 149–152
    antifouling paints 150
    engine noise 151
    sewage emission 42
    sewage treatment 151
property, passing of (new yacht) 34
Property Services Agency 82, 128
protests 67

rabies 67
racing yachts 67, 71–72, 82
radio-telephone Ships' Licence 144
Ramsar sites 82
rates, mooring 80
rating of moorings
    valuation officer 143
Receiver of Wreck 112
Red Ensign 10
Registrar General of Shipping 21
registration 5, 21
    certificate 25, 144
    qualifications 6
registration, requirement to 1
    of mortgages 12
    Small Ships Register 11
regulations – construction and
    equipment 39
Remainder Waterways 86 .
repairers, consumer protection 50
riggers, consumer protection 50
risk, passing of 18
rivers, public rights of navigation 83
RNLI, salvage 114
Royal Navy, salvage 114
Royal Society for the Protection of Birds
    81

RYA 28, 45, 49, 50, 62, 68, 147

sailmakers, consumer protection 50
Sale of Goods Act 1979 18, 26, 28, 29, 52
salvage 111–121
    agreement 119
    aircraft 112
    award 117–119
    high seas 111
    limitation of liability 74
    non-tidal water 115
    Receiver of wreck 112
    salvors lien 15, 116
    towing 113
selling a second-hand yacht 12
sewage discharges 151
sharing a yacht 4
Sites of Special Scientific Interest (SSI)
    82
Small Craft Directive
    European Commission 48
Small Ships Register (SSR) 11, 22
solicitors 60
special protection areas 82
speed limits 127
suppliers, consumer protection 50
Supply of Goods & Services Act 1979 55
survey 17, 19
surveyor 60
syndicate ownership 4

title 19
trailing 153–162
    brakes 158–159
    height 155
    insurance 154
    length 154
    lighting 160–162
    overhangs 156
    projections 156
    safe load 154
    suspension 159
    tyres 159
    weight 157–158
    width 155
tonnage measurement 6
Trade Descriptions Act 1968 59
Transport, Department of 1, 78
    commercially used pleasure craft 43,
        47
    load lines 43, 44
    passenger certificate 40
Transport and Works Act 1992
trespass by mooring 78
Trinity House 64, 132

Unfair Contract Terms Act 1979 56, 58
unregistered mortgages 12, 22

valuation (insurance) 96
Valuation Officer
  rating of moorings 143
Value Added Tax 15, 16, 22, 23, 24, 36,
  37, 144

vehicle insurance 154

warranties on sale of yacht 18, 26
windsurfers 127

YBDSA 19, 45